Planetary Transition

DIVALDO FRANCO
BY THE SPIRIT MANOEL PHILOMENO DE MIRANDA

PLANETARY TRANSITION

LEAL Publisher

Copyright© 2016 by
Centro Espírita Caminho da Redenção – Salvador (BA) – Brazil

All rights reserved. No part of this book may be reproduced by any mechanical, photographic, or electronic process, or in the form of a phonographic recording; nor may it be stored in a retrieval system, transmitted, or otherwise be copied for public or private use without prior written permission of the publisher.

ISBN: 978-1-942408-47-5

Original title in Portuguese:
Transição Planetária
(Brazil, 2010)

Translated by: Darrel W. Kimble, Marcia Saiz and Ily Reis
Cover design by: Cláudio Urpia
Layout: Luciano Carneiro Holanda
Edited by: Evelyn Yuri Furuta

Edition of
LEAL PUBLISHER
8425 Biscayne Blvd. Suite 104
Miami, Florida 33138, USA
www.lealpublisher.com
info@lealpublisher.com
(305) 306-6447

Authorized edition by Centro Espírita Caminho da Redenção – Salvador (BA) – Brazil

INTERNATIONAL DATA FOR CATALOGING IN PUBLICATION (ICP)

f825	Miranda, Manoel Philomeno de (Spirit). *Planetary Transition* / authored by the Spirit Manoel Philomeno de Miranda; psychographed by Divaldo Pereira Franco ; translated by Darrel Kimble, Marcia Saiz and Ily Reis – Miami (FL), USA : Leal Publisher, 2016.
	
	 240 p. ; 21 cm
	
	 Original title: Transição Planetária
	
	 ISBN 978-1-942408-47-5
	
	 1. Spiritism. 2. Manoel Philomeno de Miranda. 3. Revelation I. Franco, Divaldo Pereira, 1927-. II. Title.
	                                                        CDD 133.9
	                                                        CDU 133.7

Contents

Planetary Transition 9
1. New Pathways 17
2. A Special Visitor 25
3. A Revelation-Message 31
4. Earthly Itineraries 41
5. New Experiences 49
6. The Work of Illumination 59
7. Love as Divine Power 67
8. Unexpected Assistance 73
9. Existential Challenges 81
10. Lessons of High Magnitude 89
11. Continued Learning 97
12. Life Responds as Planned 107
13. Making up for Lost Time 117
14. Guidelines for the Future 133
15. Enlightening Experiences 143
16. Reincarnation Programming 155
17. Broadening the Scope of Our Work 171
18. Thoughts and Profound Dialogues 183
19. Getting Ready for Spiritual Armageddon 195

20. Confrontation with the Darkness 205
21. Difficult Battles 217
22. Preparations for the Conclusion of Our Work 229
    Ivon Costa 239

In order for people to be happy on the earth, it must be populated only by good incarnate and discarnate spirits who desire nothing but the good. Once such a time has come, there will be a great emigration from among those who inhabit the earth. Those who practice evil for evil's sake and are untouched by the sentiment of the good will no longer be worthy of the transformed planet. They will be banished from it, because their stay would once more cause trouble and confusion and would be an obstacle to progress. ... They will be replaced by more-advanced spirits, who will see to it that justice, peace and fraternity reign.

...The present age is one of transition; the members of both generations are mixed together. Standing at the midpoint, we are watching the departure of one and the arrival of the other, and each is already distinguishable by the characteristics that are proper to it.

KARDEC, ALLAN, *GENESIS*
Chapter XVIII, Nos. 27 and 28
(International Spiritist Council, 2009)

Planetary Transition

We are living on earth at the time of the great transition from a world of trials and expiations to a world of regeneration.

The changes being observed are of a moral nature, inviting human beings to change their behavior for the better, dropping their bad habits so that the paradigms of justice, duty, love, and order may take root.

This transformation, inherent in the process of evolution, has been foretold ever since the prophetic Sermon recorded in the 13th chapter of the Gospel of Mark, when the Divine Master described the signs of future times after the painful events that would indicate the different periods of evolution.

Since human beings are spirits in the process of intellectual and moral growth, they go through different levels in order to develop instinct and then intelligence, followed by consciousness on the pathway to intuition, which will be acquired by overcoming primeval experiences. These experiences affect them profoundly, often binding them to their animal nature to the detriment of their spiritual nature, which is their reality.

Through many reincarnations they very gradually eliminate their moral imperfections and transform them into *important qualities that drive them toward the wholeness for which they are destined.*

Committing wrongs and correcting them, making attempts at progress, falling and then getting back up – such is the means of growth that propels everyone in the direction of their complete happiness.

Heirs to the conflicts that afflicted them in the early stages, they must face unhealthy conditionings and work to acquire new experiences that comprise sure guidelines for further advancement.

Faced with critical situations on the carnal pathway that generate emotional complications – because they are still far from the sublime emotions of love and thus act more by their instincts, especially those that concern the preservation of life, reproduction and violence for the automatic defense of bodily existence – they attack, when they should dialogue, and they accuse, when it would be best to silence the offense or aggression, giving rise to unfortunate clashes that cause resentment, hatred, and the desire for revenge – those inconsequential children of the domineering ego.

Due to the inherent drive that impels individuals toward God, the demand for progress is unwavering, a necessity for breaking free of the strong shackles that hold them back.

Placed by the power of determinism within the context of free will – which is not always logical – only the impact of suffering awakens them to understand just how essential it is to acquire peace and well-being... At that moment they notice the wrongs they have committed and the harm they have caused others. The longing to make amends surfaces and they assist those who have been harmed by their ineptitude or primitivism in relation to the duties that are part of the sovereign codes of the ethics of life.

Planetary Transition

Hesitating or advancing on the liberating pathway, they develop the treasures lying dormant in the mind and the sentiments, which they learn to put in the service of progress, advancing, conscious of their responsibilities.

Unfortunately, this awakening to consciousness has occurred very slowly, giving rise to excesses repeated at every moment, as well as terrible, bloody wars.

Thus, arbitrary and perverse behaviors predominate in today's society, in stark contrast to the technological and scientific acquisitions realized over time.

One can often notice the harbingers of good sentiments when someone is the victim of a fateful circumstance, setting relief groups in motion, at a time when other individuals make themselves into human bombs, cowardly and fanatically murdering others who have nothing to do with the tragedies they intend to remedy by such sinister and inadequate means that are worse than the individuals whom they intend to fight...

Animal protection movements are sensitizing many segments of society, while countless people remain indifferent to millions of children, elderly and sick individuals who die of hunger every year, not for lack of food that the planet provides, but due to a total lack of compassion and solidarity...

Terrifying seismic phenomena frequently shake the planet, awakening the sympathy of other nations toward those that have been struck, while, at the same time, so-called smart weapons reap hundreds and thousands of lives, in the service of war, endless revolutions, or crimes by organizations dedicated to evil...

These are the paradoxes of societal life, which the great transition now taking place on the planet will change.

Those who have persisted in wrongful indifference to the pain of their neighbor; those who have lived their lives in known or unknown crime; those who have signed pacts involving extortion, bribery and so-called white-collar crimes, displaying egotistical behavior, gloating about the afflictions of others, taking pleasure in lust and addiction, in the undue exploitation of other lives – these will not be able to remain on the earth any longer, but will be exiled to lower worlds, where they will be useful, filing the edges of their moral imperfections, to return later to the generous bosom of Mother Earth, whom they do not want to respect today.

The eminent codifier of Spiritism,[1] assisted by Voices from Heaven, dwelled more than once on analyzing the tragic events that would shake the earth and its inhabitants in order to awaken them to their responsibilities towards themselves and their planet.

In *The Spirits' Book*, in the chapter on the Law of Destruction, the illustrious master of Lyon addresses the causes and reasons for the imbalances that frequently occur on the planet, occasioning collective tragedies, as well as those produced by humans, and he shows that it is necessary that everything be destroyed in order to be renewed. Destruction, however, is only produced for the molecular modification of matter; it never reaches the spirit, which is immortal.

Thus, major disasters of this or that origin are meant to invite human beings to reflect on the transitoriness of the carnal journey when compared to their immortality.

The suffering that derives from these so-called destructive calamities aims to "... force [humankind] to progress more quickly. Have we not stated that destruction is necessary

---

[1] Allan Kardec (1804-1869). – I. R.

for the moral regeneration of spirits, who accomplish a new degree of perfection during each new existence? You must see the end in order to appreciate the results. You only judge such things from your own personal point of view, and you regard such afflictions as calamities because of the injury they cause you. However, these hardships are often necessary in order to make things arrive at a better order more quickly, and to accomplish in a few years what would otherwise require many centuries."[2]

That is what is happening today.

Suffering has reached almost unbearable levels and the madness taking its toll on the terrestrial landscape is pandemic in character, alongside depressive disorders, drug addiction, unbridled sex, monumental psychological flights from reality, staggering crimes, disregard for laws and ethics, disregard for human and animal rights and the rights of nature... Maximum imbalance has been reached, facilitating divine interference so that the great transformation that we all so urgently need may be implemented.

Contributing to the great work of regenerating humanity, spirits from another dimension are plunging into the terrestrial darkness so that, alongside noble missionaries of love and charity, intelligence and sentiment, who protect terrestrial beings, they may modify the landscapes of affliction and enable the establishment of God's Kingdom *in people's hearts.*

We realize that our information may cause astonishment in some scholars of Spiritism, and even severe reactions in others... Nonetheless, please allow us to present our thoughts after having lived with high-order mentors who are working in the lofty program of the great transition...

---

[2] Kardec, Allan, *The Spirits' Book*, no. 737 – Spirit Auth. [International Spiritist Council, 4th ed. 2010, p. 422]. – Spirit Auth.

In order to improve the current psychosphere, thereby facilitating the work of the Messengers of Jesus, teams of apostles of charity on the spirit plane are also descending to the suffering planet in order to contribute to the changes that must occur, attending to those who experience the excruciation of violent or unexpected discarnation, who suffer under the yoke of cruel obsessions, or who are mired in unjustifiable rebelliousness, considering themselves to be opponents of the Light and members of the fury of Evil.

In this book, we describe three distinct but interpenetrating phases concerning the work to which we have been called – thanks to the compassion of Love – so that we may accompany the ennobling activities of worthy and valiant Benefactors connected to the program in progress regarding the planetary transition that has been underway for quite some time now...

We have no other goal than to encourage the servants of the Good to continue their ministry at any cost, without discouragement or annoyance, remaining confident that they are supported in all situations, as painful as they may be.

We have sought to summarize relief operations to discarnates victimized by the devastating tsunami that hit the Indian Ocean, causing tragic consequences that continue to cause suffering and pain, especially since it is being followed by many others that have been occurring with frightening frequency...

Next, we refer to the special contribution of spirits dedicated to the task involving the reincarnations of new workers, whether from the earth or volunteers from another cosmic dimension. Then, we analyze the torments that are invading the earth, as well as the interference of low-order spirits, who delight in maintaining the terrible current state of confusion.

Nonetheless, at all times, we aim to demonstrate the providential mercy of Jesus, ever watchful with His messengers over all planetary occurrences, minimizing human afflictions and opening the way to the radiant day of tomorrow approaching with a wealth of blessings and wholeness.

Thanking the Lord of our lives and the high-order spirits invested in the sublime task of the great planetary transition for having granted us the honor to work at their side, I am their devoted servant forever.

MANOEL PHILOMENO DE MIRANDA
Salvador, Brazil, April 9, 2010

1
New Pathways

As the bustle decreased with the arrival of dusk, followed by a night gently lit by stellar pendants, a psychosphere of peace engulfed the area all around Oscar and me.

Activities in our community continued in the blessed rhythm of multiple endeavors of love and relief, of education and moral development.

Groups of industrious spirits were leaving for the earth on special endeavors, while others were returning jubilant after having completed theirs.

The education and whole health departments were still at work, whereas activity in *Colônia Redenção*[3] decreased so that residents could return to their homes or go to specialized learning centers, maintaining a climate of harmony all around.

Nature in celebration touched the colony with a gentle breeze perfumed by flowers blooming in the garden from where we were observing Mother Earth adorned with artificial lights, which off in the distance seemed like coruscating diamonds embedded in the velvety navy-blue quilt that enveloped her.

---

[3] Redemption Colony, located in the spirit world. – I.R.

We had been silent for a little while after discussing the latest events shaking earthly society after the tsunami that had resulted from the clash of tectonic plates in the abyss of the Indian Ocean.

We had learned of the staggering death toll while gathered in prayer for the defenseless victims of the seismic tragedy.

Our community's administration had deployed two hundred discarnate experts to work with the Guides of Humanity, assisting those that had been hit by the fury of the gigantic waves and their consequences.

We had discussed the survivors, marked by overwhelming pain, by the epidemics that had already struck the region where the bodies were decomposing, by the misery resulting from material losses, and by the unspeakable longing for loved ones who had been snatched away by death.

The most heartrending phase was underway during those days, when the cruel consequences of misfortune were shattering the sentiments of the discouraged and bewildered survivors...

We had had the opportunity to witness the terrifying scenes very accurately projected in our auditorium, moving us all to tears.

We had also been touched by the activity and interest of civilized countries providing immediate help, all contributing with invaluable collaboration capable of mitigating the suffering whipping the victims, some still dazed by the violent jolts, and others almost insane from despair and hopelessness.

We knew that thousands of high-order spirits had flocked to their aid, striving to rescue them from unfortunate, vampirizing spirits eager for the vital fluids of the recently discarnate victims.

At the same time, we had been informed about the measures being taken to decrease the behavioral disorders that were spreading amongst those that had remained behind in their garbs of flesh...

Off in the distance, the earth moved almost imperceptibly in the infinite ocean of *cosmic musicality*.

Various emotions took ahold of both of us, enabling us to express sentiments of love and tenderness for beloved Gaia – the Earth – beautiful, magical and suffering in her few-billion year odyssey to become the happy home of a few billion inhabitants that depended on her resources for their moral and spiritual ascension.

How much we owe you! – we reflected.

How many more lifetimes would be necessary for us in the future to make it a *planet of regeneration*?

At the same time – I wondered silently – how much pain would have to afflict people's hearts for there to be a change in their mental, moral and emotional conduct to render them worthy of being liberated from the sickly legacies of the past so that the *Kingdom of Heaven* within them might be ushered in?

Meanwhile, soft music reached our ears from the nearby sanctuary where they were rehearsing Johann Sebastian Bach's *Mass in B Minor*, originally composed for orchestra, but performed there on a masterfully played organ accompanying our community's children's choir...

We were experiencing the feeling that Heaven itself was communicating with our colony at that very moment.

In fact, that was actually the case because the building reserved for celebrations of love and religious faith was illuminated with soft, silvery-blue tonalities. I was particularly impressed by the movement of the sound waves, which obeyed the sweet, gentle rhythm of the organ and children's voices.

Almost ecstatic, I was about to say something to my friend Oscar, when I noticed he was weeping discretely.

In our perfect, spontaneous mental oneness, I could see him thinking in retrospect about when, as a child living in the Austrian Alps, he had been in the wooden village chapel listening to the same composition on an old organ...

His memories increased and the scenery changed. I saw him running through the green meadows in an area marked by painted wooden houses amid mountains covered with *eternal ice*, the ground dotted with tiny flowers mixed in with colorful poppies and roses in the green grass...

My dear friend's evocative kaleidoscope was projected onto my mental screen, prompting me to recall my own childhood dominated by the scenery of sunny, joyful Bahia, Brazil, where the Lord of Life had honored me with my most recent reincarnation.

Lulled by the sublime melody, the whole mystical magic of that kindly people, their simplicity and resigned suffering – especially those of indigenous and African descent – their hopes and aspirations, pervaded my spirit.

I could not tell the time that had elapsed as the night advanced.

As we came back to reality, my friend and I seemed to have awakened from a happy dream, and almost without realizing it, we had joined hands, smiling and thanking God.

I could tell that Oscar was aware of my psychic perception of his memories, to which he immediately responded:

"Actually, I was born in a beautiful region of Tyrol, in a green valley in the Austrian Alps. I was of Jewish descent, but because there was no synagogue in our region, I was allowed to participate in the study of the Catholic Catechism and attend a beautiful little village church. My parents, true angels of the Lord, did not force us to keep our ancestral faith or prevent us from taking part in the incomparable lessons of Jesus with the other children.

"My mother was a teacher and my father a doctor, fully dedicated to the good of the humble community.

"After the invasion of Austria, our home was ransacked by soldiers of the SS on an unforgettable night of horror. We were dragged out and thrown into a police van that took us to Vienna. From there, we were loaded into an overcrowded train to a concentration camp of forced labor and extermination in Auschwitz as part of Hitler's *final solution*, designed and carried out by Himmler and his minions...

"Needless to say, when we arrived at the camp, and after the men, women, elderly, sick and children were separated my parents were sent to the gas chamber and subsequently thrown into the cremation ovens."

He made a natural pause and I suggested that he not recall the evil event.

With a slow, sad voice, he told me that he was doing so as a catharsis to release him from deep fixations...

He continued:

"Since I was over 16 years old, I was spared for forced labor alongside other living dead who moved about automatically, trying to stay alive.

"After two years of sheer horror, I was transferred to another no less cruel camp – Sobibor, part of the Heinhard operation, whereupon, thankfully, the war ended and we were freed...

"I was taken to a refugee camp in Austria, in spite of the near total destruction of Vienna. God had allowed me the honor of surviving the Holocaust and I restarted my invaluable human experience...

"Deeply marked by physical and emotional pain, experiencing nights of nightmares that seemed to never end, I opted for celibacy. I didn't want to disturb the dear soul who might marry me.

"In tribute to my parents and the victims of the extermination, I began to attend the Synagogue, but, almost paradoxically, I didn't lose my love for Jesus...

"I pursued an education and graduated in Medicine at the University of Vienna, and within my moral background, I devoted myself to the missionary practice of that science responsible for combating diseases and suffering...

"I returned to the *Great Home*[4] at fifty years of age and began living in a Jewish spirit community with my parents, having been summoned to the activity that we must attend to as brothers and sisters in humanity."

He smiled with a thin veil of sadness on his face and held out his hand to me, emotionally pronouncing the Hebrew word *Shalom* (Peace).

Now smiling, he exclaimed:

"New pathways!"

"New pathways!" I replied, euphoric.

---

[4] Spirit World. – I.R.

We were to return to our beloved Mother Earth for special activities, in accordance with the program prepared by Benefactors in our community.

Highly touched and thankful to the Lord for such reflections and emotions, we said goodbye to each other and headed for our rooms.

New pathways! I went home thinking about the seriousness of the endeavors to be undertaken. I soon concluded that the Lord would give us His support and inspiration since they would be carried out in His name.

2
A Special Visitor

We had been told that our community would be visited by a high-order spirit, the resident of another dimension. He would bring us invaluable news about future activities to be carried out shortly on the earth, and in which Oscar and I would be involved.

Hence the day had passed marked by sweet expectations.

That night, at the agreed time, with the skies embroidered with stellar diamonds, the two of us headed for the place dedicated to special conferences.

It was a semi-circular building surrounded by well-tended gardens highlighted by lush trees and lit fountains whose waters danced in the air to the sound of delightful melodies. It was in a broad area in the heart of the colony.

The room reserved for events of this magnitude held two thousand specially invited persons. There were other, smaller rooms, however, for smaller, specialized meetings. These were duly equipped with technological means that would afford a better understanding of the topics.

The upper dome of the building was composed of transparent material, allowing one to see the dark velvet of the night with its flaming silvery pendants.

There was a perfect view from every spot in the elegant auditorium, inviting one to meditate and journey within...

The psychosphere resulting from activities held there regularly hovered in the environment.

Gradually, either silently or in quiet conversation, the comfortable seats were filling up with those waiting for the event to start.

Just before 8:00 p.m. – according to terrestrial clocks – the room was full.

Our Governor General entered with other members responsible for our community, indicating the high significance of the event.

We had received vague information about Orion, who would come to us from the constellation Taurus – particularly, from one of the Pleiades – in order to present us with important information regarding the momentous project involving en masse reincarnations that had been taking place on our beloved planet since the second half of the last century, incarnations that were now intensifying.

The featured table at the front of the auditorium rested on a platform placed in such a way as to be clearly visible to everyone present.

Before the members that would sit at it were invited to do so, the children's choir sang the *Miserere* – also called the *Penance* – which refers to Psalm 51. It was originally composed by Gregorio Allegri, but in the 18th century a still very young Mozart heard it for the first time, memorized it and adapted it with minor changes.

The beautiful music begins with a prayer: *Lord, have mercy on me*, and continues, movingly, characterized by repentance for wrongs committed, and rich in the certainty of divine love...

Emotions took us all as the angelic voices prayed for compassion for our imperfections as we followed along in a prayerful state.

Profound silence ensued, after which the master of ceremonies called the administrator and a number of other invaluable leaders to complete the table.

Next, he asked the spirit Ivon Costa, the selfless spreader of Spiritism in Brazil during the first half of the last century, to say the opening prayer.

I noticed that on one side of the table sat two female spirits wearing long, white vaporous robes. They were next to a tube made of tenuous light coming down from the ceiling...

With a melodious voice like a skillfully played flute, Ivon Costa, visibly inspired, stood in prayer, which we followed silently:

Jesus, our Benefactor!
While our beloved planet agonizes in its process of evolutionary growth, suffering harsh trials and expiations, dragging its inhabitants toward untold sufferings, we who love you are gathered here to pray for your mercy in the face of the moral inferiority that rules our spiritual nature.

For millennia you have summoned us to build the spiritual kingdom in our minds and hearts, though we have failed to properly answer your call.

In ancient cultures and civilizations, starting at the time of the Sumerians, a few of us realized the lofty meaning of earthly existence, but we let ourselves be anesthetized by the deceitful vapors of matter...

Later, in Persia and Nineveh we learned the Truth and its mysteries, but quickly abandoned them to follow the warring mobs of Darius or Shalmaneser, conquering lands and spreading death. Ours was the sowing of blood, orphanhood, widowhood and hatred, and our reaping was bitter, unnamed pain in Babylon and in Egypt, which fascinated us with its ostentatious temples, dragging us afterward to bloody defeats with Astyages and the murder of Akhenaten...

We traveled the mountains of Tibet and the plains of India, repeating the lessons of the Mahabharata, which thrilled us, but we were unable to change our unfortunate bellicosity...

Venerable China, with Fo-Hi, among other philosophers, taught us wisdom, but it did not quench our insane thirst for power over Manchuria and its neighboring peoples, who also destroyed it several times with their chariots of destruction...

We crossed the desert with Moses, as we would do at a later time with Ezra – thanks to the noble Cyrus – to rebuild the Temple and Jerusalem. We attacked the Philistines and other peoples, sowing terror, condemning, destroying...

Athens charmed us starting in the days of Anaxagoras, and then with the lessons of Socrates, but in Sparta what we had learned from them did not keep us from handing ourselves over to heinousness and unceasing battles...

We accompanied Scipio, the African, as we had done with Alexander the Great, the Macedonian, and Hannibal, the Carthaginian, even though we knew about the philosophy of immortality and the interference of the gods in our lives...

And with You, after listening to Your lessons of incomparable beauty, we abandoned faithfulness and converted Your doctrine into lies, lust, hypocrisy and misfortune...

Thus, we crossed the medieval night, warned by martyrs and saints, attached to infamy and horror.

We died and were reborn countless times before truly awakening to life in abundance when the light of Spiritism seized us from dense inner darkness, from ignorance and from the abyss of egotistical madness...

There was a pause filled with emotion. We were all breathing in rhythm with the evocative, profound and serious narration.

Ivon continued with the same tone of voice and the same emotion:

More than once Your mercy has shaken the planetary ship, as occurred just recently with the tsunami, demonstrating the weakness of human devices and their sparse possibilities of knowing God's will so that all may finally wake up.

Once again You have asked for the support of other spirits for the great transition that will take place soon in the physical world.

Now, enable the Ambassador from another sphere to bring us Your blessing in the name of universal love so that we may consciously serve You with discernment and dedication.

We are here, on our knees and expectant, at Your service, with heart and mind open to the truth.

Have mercy, O Lord!

When he finished, the materialization of the special guest in the tube of light was complete, thanks to the contribution of the mediums who offered him the proper substance for the event.

He was slightly taller than the earthly standard. His eyes looked like two flaming stars in the sky of a kindly face. His bodily movements were harmonious when he left the place where he had condensed and followed the master of ceremonies, who led him to a special, distinguished seat on the platform.

A soft, sweet scent engulfed the immense auditorium and we all concentrated on the venerable guest.

Again the children's choir endeared us with their sublime singing.

3
A Revelation-Message

We had not yet emerged from our near-ecstasy, when our leader approached the distinguished visitor and greeted him with deference and affection.

He then led him to the podium and gave him the floor.

The noble spirit thanked him with a cheerful smile and began his speech:

"Venerable administrators, fraternal souls of all dimensions:

"We greet you all in the name of the Lord of the Universe.

"Representing the beautiful globe of love installed in one of the Pleiades, wrapped in special vibrations made of photons that form a luminosity composed of blue tones, we are here in answer to the invitation of the Sublime Governor of Planet Earth.

"Although I am not in a position to speak on behalf of our spirit Guides, I bring our commitment to contribute with you to the program of elevating humanity through the reincarnation of servants of the Good purposely prepared for the sublime endeavor.

"This is not the first time that the earth has received travelers from other *dwellings* at the request of Jesus Christ. It also happened in the past, at the time of the monumental transition of forms, when shapers of the organic vessel delved into the dense physical mass to set the characteristics that now define its inhabitants... Those noble ambassadors of the light came from the constellation Auriga to contribute to the construction of present humanity, including other non-moralized intelligences, who, after having concluded a number of evolutionary stages, happily returned to their own beloved homes...

"At other times, luminaries of the Truth immersed themselves in the darkness of the terrestrial world in order to offer their uplifting achievements and accomplishments, helping its inhabitants to grow in technology, science, philosophy, religion, politics, ethics and morals... Nonetheless, most of the development occurred in the area of intelligence and not sentiment, which explains its current stage of evolution: rich in knowledge but poor in spiritual virtues...

"Moreover, the planet periodically experiences climate changes and widespread seismic events that cause profound changes in its immense mass, or it suffers the impact of meteors that alter its structure, making it more beautiful and harmonious. All these occasional destructions are always intended for progress, thus obeying a higher plan to take it to the level of a *world of regeneration*.

"Concurrently, in order to be able to travel on the great earthly ship as it advances morally through the landscapes of happy orbs, countless members of the barbarian tribes of the past, who had been held in special regions for centuries, so as not to impede the planet's development, are being reborn with lovely organic constitutions, the results of natural genetic selection, though marked by remnants of primitivism.

"Some appear exotic; others, aggressive, seeking their primeval origins in unconscious reaction against progressive society, but having the holy opportunity to reshape their ideas, hone their sentiments and participate in the unstoppable upward march... A substantial number, however, remain aggressive and emotionally indifferent, becoming instruments of harsh trials for the society they disdain. They have an excellent opportunity, but if they squander it, they will be sent to other primitive worlds, where they will contribute their knowledge, while suffering, however, from harsh injunctions. This is a type of repeat of the Biblical exile of Lucifer and his minions to realms compatible with their unrefined emotional level, where longing and melancholy will encourage them to work for the heritage of love previously wasted on crudeness, and then fight with zeal for the conquest of the good.

"They have been here at different periods of earth's culture, enjoying luminous but rarely used chances. However, for now, their vibrational density does not allow them to be reborn on the new world under construction."

The Emissary paused and gazed with luminous eyes around the huge auditorium immersed in silence and reflection, absorbing his every word. He continued:

"The *mansions of the Father* are infinite in number and there is constant communication amongst their members so as to preserve the sublime fraternity, for those who are more enlightened must contribute on behalf of those less knowledgeable at the moment. The sublime law of exchange entails a high level of spiritual content.

"Just as millions of high-order spirits will descend from our sphere to the earth – as is already happening – for the inevitable confrontation between selfless love and destructive violence, giving way to clashes characterized by mercy and compassion, other missionaries of education and solidarity, who strove to promote them in previous lives, will also return, contributing from birth to the construction of the new mentality, thus helping to speed up the changes that are already occurring...

"In this way, earthly consciousness and human genetics are able to receive new guests, who will participate in the illuminative agape – to which the eminent Codifier of Spiritism referred in his magisterial work *Genesis* – consisting of all those who love the truth and endeavor to grow spiritually, laboring on behalf of others and society as a whole.

"Thus, as happens on other orbs, the time has come for your Mother Earth to also ascend the scale of worlds, taking her children with her and awaiting the return of those who will be in the rearguard for some time to come, for the ineffable love of God leaves no one helpless, but provides them with the opportunity to remake themselves and evolve.

"We are all committed to this inevitable effort, experiencing love in all its expressions, forming a harmonious and charming contingent.

"No one can escape this duty, because it belongs to everyone, both individually and collectively, for the Kingdom of Heaven is within us and it is necessary to expand its borders to the outside, making way for the longed-for

Paradise, even though it will never be within the territorial limits of physical organization.

"Our reality as immortal spirits in essence has its origin and residence outside the material limitations of any physical world, which could not even exist without causing any obstacle to the process of evolution. Nonetheless, when the Creator established the need for development in physiological organizations, like the seed that needs mesological conditions to release the life lying within it, there are convincing grounds for such to happen, enabling us to go through the steps that lead us to the Infinite..."

Again he paused, allowing us to reflect and internalize the information, some of it somewhat familiar and some of it quite new, while distinctive waves of peace and joy vibrated all around.

Looking around us, we noticed faces sweetly wrapped in subtle light arising from the joy they felt, and from the hope that they too could contribute to the New Era.

He continued with the same musical tone:

"Hence, why should spirits come from another Orb to help moralize your planet? First, having no previous ties arising from perturbing existences, they would not have to confront inner impediments to the benevolent giving processes or the painful reencounters with those who remain committed to evil, who have an interest in maintaining the moral backwardness of communities in order to exploit them psychically in perverse phenomena of vampirization, of individual and collective obsessions... *Strangers* in lands ready for progress, they do it out of love, called to offer their values obtained in other realms, facilitating access to the development of those who are *natives* longing for happiness.

Second, because the ones that are more advanced morally can contribute edifying examples capable of silencing the forces of evil and obstructing them with unsurpassed resources of personal sacrifice, since their aspirations are not immediate and self-serving in the world of forms. While others will be experiencing a form of temporary exile in that they are developed intellectually but still inexperienced in the realm of love, in direct contact with the less evolved they will feel the need for affection and caring, learning, in turn, the miraculous phenomenon of solidarity. Everything, therefore, is summarized in giving, which means receiving, and in receiving, which invites giving.

"In order for the program to be carried out, at this very moment brothers and sisters from our planet are introducing the same program in other spirit communities near the earth so that together we may form a single caravan of industrious servants, attending to the orders of the terrestrial Governor, its Master par excellence.

"Spirit groups prepared for disseminating the program will leave from all these communities to communicate with serious Spiritist institutions, calling their members to divulge guidelines for the new commitments.

"Dedicated speakers and sincere mediums will be invited to participate in preparatory studies and seminars in order to trigger an international action on the planet, inviting serious people to contribute psychically and morally to the new era.

"Although great changes are taking place in phases of upheaval due to climatic phenomena, pollution and disregard for nature, they will not occur in the form of destruction of life, but in a change in people's moral and emotional behavior. Some will be called to change while suffering through these occurrences; others through their discernment with respect to evolution.

"Just as the ocean waves voluptuously embrace the beaches that absorb their white foam, the new workers of the Lord will continuously change social habits, moral customs, literature, art, general knowledge, science and technology, imprinting new texts of beauty that will awaken the interest of even those who are asleep for now.

"But before reaching that point, violence, sensuality, abjection, scandals and corruption will reach unheard-of levels, reaching the bottom of the well while degenerative illnesses, bipolar disorders, heart diseases, cancers, addictions and sexual deviances will cry out for peace, for a return to ethics, morals, and balance… Fruits of people's passions, who will suffer their effects in the form of liberating infirmities, the values of full health, flawless joy, personal harmony and integration into the cosmic spirit of life will slowly arise.

"As in any battle, difficult moments will arise, requiring balance and prayer; the combatants will be exposed to the world, misunderstood, challenged for acting differently, and for making the foolish uncomfortable, who, in their inability to emulate them, will fight them. They will suffer many bouts of profound and apparent loneliness, but they will never, ever be alone, because the spiritual solidarity of Love will be with them, energizing them and encouraging them to carry on.

"Being on the vanguard always tests the moral endurance of those that dare to be different in order to evolve, when vulgarity predominates all around, the reason why all those dedicated to illuminative and liberating experiences are so special. They should never be afraid, however. The Spirit of the Lord will animate them, giving them unknown joy of living, even when there seems to be a conspiracy against their lofty purposes.

"The model to follow is still Jesus, and the new wave of love will bring the return of the apostolate, the unforgettable days of the persecutions and martyrdom, which, at present, have different characteristics since their bodies cannot be killed with impunity as in the past... This does not mean they will not suffer shameful accusations or that demoralizing campaigns will not be promoted against them in order to hinder their lofty endeavors. Nevertheless, they must move forward, joyful and stoic, singing hymns of freedom and rational faith that dignify human beings and promote inner growth.

"It is, therefore, a movement that will change the planet for the better in order to help it reach the level reserved for it.

"Those who do join the struggle and participate in the movement will be candidates for isolation and death...

"Thus, under the command of the Songbook of the Beatitudes, let us press on, engaged in genuine fraternity, offering ourselves in a sacrifice of love for the truth, certain of the success for which we are destined.

"Therefore, praising the one who invited us, let us pray for mercy."

He finished his eloquent speech with tears in his eyes...

The Governor General of our community approached and embraced him affectionately – something we all wanted to do.

Again, the children's choir sang a romantic ballad, totally unknown to me, while delicate rose petals fell upon us all, dissolving upon contact and giving off a special fragrance.

Immediately thereafter, conducted by our administrator, the emissary returned to the tube of light and vanished.

He had fulfilled the duty that brought him to our colony.

The master of ceremonies went over to the podium and ended the solemnity.

We all rose slowly in silence, forming small groups interested in discussing the speech, while others, like us, approached the platform to converse with the noble members of our community and put ourselves at their disposal.

When Ivon Costa recognized us, he also approached our governor and a long and edifying conversation ensued.

The comments continued for a few minutes until, like the other workers, the three of us – Oscar, Ivon, and myself – headed back to our quarters.

4
EARTHLY ITINERARIES

For me personally, that had been a very special night. As I thought about the message concerning humankind's future, I could not contain the ineffable joy of living at such a meaningful time: the construction of the New Era.

Since the remote pages of the Gospels, as well as the narrations in the Book of Revelation – and even earlier – there are prophesies about the earth being a happy world after the terrible scourges that would impact creatures and the lacerations the planet would suffer.

The strings of events that have astounded society, inviting it to ponder the convulsions that shake the physical world periodically, in addition to the heinous acts of terrorism and atrocity, are unmistakable signs that a huge change is taking place.

However, now that the first moments exploited by the tragedy-hungry media were over, other facts were becoming important, replacing those that deserve more study and mental probing in order to find solutions to the terrible effects of air pollution and the poisoning of sources of life on the planet... It is true that a number of movements were calling for corrupt nations and governments to take responsibility for the emissions of poisonous gases, while designs for global entertainment and new achievements for enjoyment and delusion were taking shape.

The tears in the victims' eyes had not yet dried, nor had the tragic effects of the events diminished, and charitable contributions had already begun to be diverted for ignoble purposes, while the sufferers beheld the indifference with which they were being treated, relegated to their own devices after the tragedy.

The beaches of several countries in the Indian Ocean were strewn with corpses, tens of thousands lay beneath the rubble of destroyed buildings, and insensitive tourist agencies were already planning new *packages* for other havens and places of leisure and perversion that had not been damaged...

Fortunately, upstanding men and women, and humanitarian organizations and entities sensitive to the pain of their neighbors rushed to generously offer resources that could lessen the despair of the victims and survivors who needed to rebuild homes and continue the human experience.

The spiritual spectacle in the affected regions, however, was very serious. Likewise, due to the decomposition of human and animal corpses and the absence of drinking water, the emergence of epidemics was a real threat, and spirits abruptly torn from their bodies were wandering, lost and desperate, around the areas where they had died. These areas had become garbage and debris fields on a heavy and menacing night without end. The cries of despair, the calls for help and the phenomena of magnetization with other unfortunate discarnates constituted the extra-physical geography of the dreadful events.

We were witnessing the sad events from our community through special means that broadcast the terrible images to us as we pondered how it might be possible to alleviate such despair and help restore order.

Banditry took advantage of the deplorable situation to repress its victims. Cunning exploiters bargained over the spoils of the lost and displaced, and heinous conspiracies forged skillful maneuvers to extract the rest from those who had almost nothing left.

Such was, in various forms, the horrid post-tragedy spectacle of the *tsunami*.

The next day, we were to meet with organizers of a trip to the embattled region so we could surmise the emergency services to be performed.

The dawn was splendid, with a turquoise blue sky glorified with soft light that illuminated our entire community.

Although we are subject to the same action of the laws that maintain the terrestrial globe, the sunlight that reaches us is always at the same temperature because there are no physical obstacles to the continuous production of heat. This also results from special layers of energy emanating from the photons that envelop our vibratory field. Thus, no changes occur like those on the planet due to its position in relation to the sun.

We were to meet at 10:00 a.m. in the shade of a venerable cedar in the yard surrounding the ecumenical temple, where those of different religious convictions can meet according to their beliefs.

The organ was emitting special music, and when Oscar and I approached, the other members surrounded us joyfully.

Ivon Costa, accompanied by the person responsible for the serious endeavor, introduced us without major formalities.

"We have the great joy," began our friend, "of introducing you to our benefactor, who is in charge of heading our earthly labors."

Our new friend smiled slightly and elaborated:

"When I was incarnate I lived most of my life in Polynesia. I was one of the conquistadors who, in the name of European civilization, imposed themselves on the islanders of a wide stretch of the southern oceans.

"We had the mistaken notion that we were superior to those whom we called 'natives,' and in the name of our false values we strove to acculturate them with our presumption of being the lords of knowledge.

"An honest mistake! The longer we lived with them, the more we discovered the wisdom in their apparent primitivism. We found, in their seemingly crude worship, profound information handed down orally from one generation to the next along with their traditional activities. Their shamans, in their momentous spirit communications, were, at the same time, priests, doctors, thinkers, scholars, counselors, administrators and effective psychologists.

"From them we learned about the interference of the *dead* in the lives of the *living,* and we also learned that the most effective therapy for facing the challenges of the health-disease binomial is always reciprocal love and care by all members of the clan.

"As time passed, I chose to live with their naivety, assimilating their customs and skills.

"My life was proving to be long and fruitful, allowing me to love unconditionally and to receive the tribute of the respect and affection of their pure sentiments.

"My discarnation did not take me away from them at all, and now, as desolation and tragedy assail those whom I owe so much, I applied to participate in one of the aid caravans to show my gratitude."

He was silent for a bit, and concluded emotionally:

"I am your brother Charles White, of English origin. I used to practice conventional medicine.

"I'm here in your colony performing an internship, for which I have brought several friends who used to wear the costumes of different nationalities. We are here in order to train special relief techniques to your guides and to apply them later in our area of work.

"It is essential that you get to know those with whom you will be carrying out an activity of love for one month, exercising solidarity in the region that awaits us on our beloved planet Earth.

"Welcome to our caravan."

Ivon introduced us to a young female spirit who served as a nursing assistant to the doctor, as well as two other dedicated workers that used to live in the Philippines.

Since we would all be together from then on embracing the responsibilities of the Good, we immediately established ties of sympathy and friendship.

"Our endeavor," Dr. White explained, "is divided into two phases. The first takes place in the region of the tsunami, and the second in the psychosphere of Brazil, preparing minds and sentiments for special reincarnations."

After explaining our project, he released us, establishing 6:00 p.m. as the time we would be leaving for our beloved planet.

Considering the magnitude of our work, curiosity piqued my mind, especially since I would be living alongside spirits of different, unfamiliar cultures and habits.

The Filipino friends introduced themselves: the older of the two informed us that he had been a Catholic priest on one of the many islands and that his name was Marcos. He had devoted himself to the ministry of the religious faith and to early childhood education. He had discarnated in 1954 at seventy years of age.

The other, younger and smiling, dressed in the manner characteristic of his people, stated that he had been a Muslim and was known as Abdul Severin. He had discarnated as a victim of malaria at 40 years of age.

Thus the caravan was composed of members of several spiritual persuasions, but we all had the point in common of understanding the love that prevails throughout the universe as one of the forces of cosmic balance, and considered to be of divine essence.

On our part, Oscar explained his Jewish background, whereas I referred to my adoption of Spiritism.

We were excited to realize we all belonged to the same flock, or as Ivon pointed out cheerfully: The Imperishable Good!

We continued our conversations while Dr. White and his assistant Anna, an Anglican, arranged the equipment necessary for the first phase of the upcoming activities.

Father Marcos, who knew the region we would be visiting, explained that the unusual and tragic clash of the tectonic plates that generated the immense, destructive waves had been expected, and that spiritual measures had been taken, including building a spiritual first-aid station above the region that had suffered the most damage from the epicenter of the disaster.

Discarnate engineers and architects had acted quickly and built an emergency outpost that would shelter us as well as those we would assist.

Interestingly, he elaborated further, stating that the vacationing Westerners who had died there had a deep emotional connection with that people and had been attracted to the area by magnetic forces to redeem old debts that weighed on their moral economy.

"Nothing happens without the foundations of causality!" he concluded.

I was surprised and asked him how he reconciled reincarnation with the Catholic dogmas he used to espouse.

Courteous and polite, he explained:

"My dear Philomeno, you know that the formulations of the Truth depart from this, the real world, for the earth, and that religions clothe them in superstitions, myths and dogmas according to the levels of awareness of the people that believe in them, concealing some and setting others free. Nonetheless, when we return to the country of immortality, such formulas disappear, giving rise to the essence, which we quickly assimilate due to affinity and the logic of the universal Good."

I smiled and we continued the uplifting conversation for two hours before starting the new endeavor.

As a phase of our spiritual growth, Ivon and I were to participate in the illuminative experience in the suffering region, accompanied by Oscar, who was an intern in our community for the same purpose.

5
New Experiences

After some time of rest and meditation, I let myself be inspired by prayer, entrusting myself to the Lord of Life with respect to our ministry with the high-order spirits whom we would soon meet on the earth.

A pleasant well-being flooded my heart and I could not hold back tears of joy and gratitude to Heaven for allowing me to learn while working, and with the example of selfless spirits.

We met at 6:00 p.m., and after a prayer by Dr. White, we boarded the special vehicle that would take us to Sumatra, Indonesia, considered the fourth most populous country on the earth, and which had been ravaged along with areas of several other countries. We were to meet up with the other groups waiting for us. More than two thirds of Indonesia had been affected by flood and destruction... Also considered to be the most populous Muslim country, its people, scattered among numerous islands (some of volcanic origin and others composed of limestone), had not grasped the magnitude of the calamity, for lack of communication.

Some high-order spirits had approached the region at the beginning of December in order to set up temporary communities to receive those who would discarnate in affliction as a result of the impending seismic event.

Having completed the trip, we arrived at the spirit community situated above the stricken area.

Although we had witnessed some of the tragedy from our colony, we could now see firsthand the damage caused by the first tidal wave and those that followed, destroying everything with the speed and Cycloptic strength of the earthquake in the deep waters of the Indian Ocean, and the destructive aftershocks that followed.

The tempestuous force had hit the coasts of India, Sri Lanka, Thailand, the Phi Islands, the Maldives, Bangladesh, and part of Africa, though with lesser effects than those that had reached other regions.

As a result, actual changes had occurred in the earth's landmass, its motion and the tilt of its axis, which, although not felt by its inhabitants, were detected by sensitive instruments.

The first tidal wave had reaped more than 150,000 lives, while successive waves, laden with the wreckage of homes, boats and buildings of all kinds, in addition to uprooted trees and boulders, sowed horror, devastating the coastal communities.

The environmental psychosphere was dense, denoting all the unmistakable signs of enormous tragedies.

We heard the clamor of frantic crowds wandering about as aimless human waves, maddened by suffering caused by the disappearance or death of loved ones and the loss of everything.

International contributions had begun arriving right away. However, aggressive instincts predominated among groups of exploiters, vagrants and criminals, who took advantage of the opportunity to pillage and terrorize.

Vibratory storms discharged dense energies on the human and geographic remains, afflicting us greatly.

Soon thereafter, we found the place that would serve as support for our forays to the planet and where other spirit relief groups were also staying. Our kindly instructor explained what we should do during those first minutes, and after he gave us instructions, we plunged into the dense night enveloping the devastated region.

Decomposing bodies were being piled up everywhere after being identified by relatives, whereas others were being moved elsewhere, calling our attention to the strong spiritual connections maintained by the newly-discarnated, who were not yet aware of what had happened. Magnetically tied to their remains, they were thrashing about, experiencing the anguish of drowning, the pain of being hit by debris, and the despair of not knowing what had happened. From time to time we heard prayers and supplications addressed to Allah, soon followed by storms of curses and blasphemies.

In a demonstration of human solidarity, a large number of incarnates were at work providing assistance, despite the dense night. Many of them had come from other countries and were experts in this type of relief. They mingled in with the caravan members from the Beyond, equally dedicated to love for one's neighbor.

Dr. White walked through the wreckage and corpses toward a group of discarnates that reminded me of a pack of hungry wolves or coyotes fighting over the remains of dead prey... The chaos was incredible, and the fist-fights between some spirits were shameful.

"They're fighting over the energies of the newly discarnate," Dr. White explained.

"With this attitude, they attack despairing newly-discarnates in an attempt to feed on their *animal energies*, starting the unfortunate process of vampirization. Identifying those who led irresponsible lives – enabling them to tune in to their vibrations – they seek to drain them, speeding up their decomposition and drawing them to regions of misery, where they will subject them to abuse and mental exploitation.

"And since they are so wretched, they vie for victims like wild animals vying for the spoils of the hunt.

"Our commitment at the moment entails removing the victims from this locale and trying to awaken them to their spiritual reality."

We approached and, at a signal from the doctor, Abdul, wearing conventional Muslim garb, raised his voice and rhythmically recited an *ayat* (verse) of one of the *Suras* (chapters) from the Koran, like a Muezzin in a minaret.

Abdul continued chanting, emitting a special and profound vibration, and suddenly there was a terrifying silence, as if the spirit brigands were snapping out of their madness. Just then, Anna approached carrying a torch that lit up the environment. She lifted it above her head and, overcome with astonishment, the *vampires* and exploiters stopped their attack.

One of them stood out with his hideous, cruel countenance, shouting that he had nothing to fear, that all should turn against the invaders and subdue them.

Abdul remained unfazed, however, and continued to recite the Book with respect and seriousness, producing a huge impact on the crazed horde.

Dr. White then explained to them what had happened shortly before, on the 26th – it was still December – starting at 8:00 a.m., and that all of them, reaped by death, needed repose; that their remains should be cremated collectively in order to avoid the diseases that follow such tragedies, some of which had already appeared.

The spirit rioters watched in obvious astonishment as Father Marcos took from the claw-like hand of one of them the spirit of a newly-deceased individual who, because the bonds of his perispirit[5] had not yet been completely severed from his physical body, was still thrashing amid the physical fluids, a state that caused this spirit inexpressible anguish, along with the terror he felt as a result of the cruel tormenter, who finally yielded to the priest's kind gesture.

Observing the ties that stretched to one of the corpses in a deplorable state of decay, the priest used counter-clockwise circular movements on the *crown chakra* to disconnect the spirit, who moaned and writhed in unspeakable agony, until the thick, putrid discharges gradually decreased and finally dissolved altogether. The discarnate spirit staggered and fainted.

Aided by Ivon, the benefactor withdrew him from the swarm and placed him some distance away in restless sleep, before continuing with another casualty.

The agitator that had been threatening Abdul ran off, abandoning the group, while the servant of the Good continued urging them to peace, respect for the victims, compassion, and mercy as recommended by his holy book.

Immediately thereafter, although the aggression of a few of the more rebellious ones continued, we copied what Father Marcos was doing and assisted some distressed sufferers who were struggling for release from the evil hands

---

[5] Kardec's terminology for what is also known as the astral body. – I.R.

exploiting them... To the degree that the connections to the corpses to which they were magnetically tied diminished, they experienced the torpor of discarnation and entered an agitated sleep state, typical of the last images received just before physical death.

Placed a short distance from the area infected by the dense, damaging spiritual fluids, groups of stretcher-bearers transferred them in silence to our temporary spirit community.

In the meantime, Abdul spoke directly with a number of obsessors and scoffers, explaining the meaning of life and the Laws that govern the universe, including, of course, the shadowy world in which they were trying to keep up the same behavior they had while alive. A moral transformation for the better was necessary so that they could truly live, freeing themselves from the fog that deadened their intelligence and deluded their sentiments.

Knowledgeable of the human soul, the skilled teacher was not intimidated by the threats of a number of hideous beings who were mocking him and the rest of us, shouting vulgar and abhorrent epithets, and threatening to fight us in defense of their interests.

Without verbally or mentally confronting them, we judiciously continued our duty, reducing the number of those who, still connected to their mangled physical bodies, were desperately trying to retake them to continue their human journey. As they finally realized this was impossible, they still could not accept the reality of it, completely losing their lucidity, throwing themselves on the ground or against each other, rebellious and weeping in agony, preventing any help from us. Thus it was urgent for there to be a point of contact that would make our job easier.

There is no violence in the Laws of love. The only thing needed is some form of identification between those in need and those predisposed to helping them.

That is why, quite often, suffering is still the best psychotherapy used by life to awaken those demented by pleasure and those devoted to cruelty.

The work was exhausting but highly meaningful because the liberation of each spirit who benefited from the gift of sleep and the immediate transfer to one of the aid sectors in our sphere meant a new path for him or her after awakening from the lethargy he or she would experience for some time.

There were moments of strife because some of the energy exploiters refused to hand over their victims to our support. They would rant and rave, ready to start a brawl. Any balanced means of action was out of the question.

Dr. White, however, communicated with us mentally, encouraging us to continue, to take advantage of the indecision of some of the persecutors, linking us to Jesus and His ministry of love to the obsessed whom He had succored. And so we continued.

The heartbreaking, unbridled screaming and the desolation all around touched us; even so, we could not mentally leave our activity in that stronghold of putrefaction and madness.

Attending to a frenzied woman holding an equally tearful and inconsolable child, I perceived that her insanity had occurred at the moment she had tried to save herself and her little girl by going up to the top part of their house until the wave tore it from its foundations, smashing it to bits and crushing both bodies in the wreckage. One could see it all recorded in her crazed mind... She could not stop screaming for help, rightly believing she was being pursued by demonic beings who wanted to subjugate her...

Touching her forehead and emitting successive waves of love and peace, I perceived that she was capturing my thoughts. Because she was open to religious faith, she could tell that I was helping both her and her daughter, and she let me take her out of the circle in which she was imprisoned, although she was still connected to her tattered body. The little one was free from the perispiritual injunction of matter and quickly quieted down upon receiving the vibrations I was sending her.

Ivon came to help out and we began to focus our attention on the bonds that kept the mother attached to her useless body. Shortly thereafter, as we managed to cut the energetic *bonds* between spirit and matter, she finally calmed down and let herself be taken while weeping poignantly, lamenting the fact that she had discarnated.

As she continued to capture our thoughts, we tried to tell her about immortality, and we reminded her of the daughter whom she should care for as if still on the earth. She should also prepare to help the rest of her family members, who, if not taken by the chariot of death, would certainly require her help in order to recover in the coming days.

When invited to think about her family, her maternal instinct grew stronger and she agreed to calm down. She managed to move, albeit with some difficulty, and hugged the little one asleep in her lap. We led her over to a group of special assistants, who would help her with arrangements compatible with her condition.

But we had not yet seen everything that human nature is capable of when the brutal forces of primitivism predominate.

We were engrossed in attending to that suffering mass, when a group of incarnates began inconsiderately removing the bodies, taking advantage of the terrible darkness of the night.

"Those are corpse robbers," Dr. White explained. "They are searching for anything of value, considering that death surprised its victims without warning as they were going about their usual affairs.

"Although the authorities are trying to bring order out of the chaos, such unfortunate exploiters resort to every means possible in order to profit from the misery of others. In removing the rotting corpses, they do not fear contamination of any nature. They put up with the terrible odors, intoxicated as they are by the alcohol they ingest and the unbridled ambition of hoarding something for degrading pleasures.

"Let's continue without paying attention to them since we are in very different vibratory fields."

6
THE WORK
OF ILLUMINATION

The hours passed, slow and heavy. The group we were assisting consisted of nearly a thousand victims of the seismic tragedy. The results of our efforts seemed insignificant, even though we were fondly doing the task that had been assigned to us.

The night was becoming increasingly fearful from the human point of view due to the ceaseless horrors.

In the physical realm, the search for bodies in order to identify them was distressing because people were weeping and cursing without any awareness as to what they were saying. It was a collective catharsis under the inclemency of the torturous darkness.

On our side, the spiritual scene was no less harrowing.

Anna kept the torch lit, spreading light across the dark and somber locale. At one point, we heard bloodcurdling howls and saw a dense formation stirring and approaching, as if pushed by gentle winds imperceptible to us... As they came near we saw several hideous spirits with wolf-like faces and forms, as if we were in a scenario of a sickly imagination, observing former human beings that had become victims of zoanthropy. With repulsive and horrid appearances, their gaping mouths were drooling and their glowing eyes were looking for bodies whose spirits we were liberating.

Suddenly, as if famished, they were about to throw themselves on one of the piles of limbs and bodies.

Dr. White signaled to Father Marcos, who quickly deployed a large web of luminous threads. Ivon and Oscar helped him toss it deftly over the stinking heap... I immediately realized it was a magnetic defense, radiating special energy that terrified the attackers, who obviously knew what it was. They quickly backed off, without further disruption of our work.

It was the first time I had encountered such a scene.

Perceiving my mental questions, the skillful director explained:

"Those were wretched spirits, whose lives on earth were awful. They constructed their current terrifying appearances as a result of the evil they practiced, indifferent to the suffering they caused. They had lost their sensitivity to love and thus they psychically deformed their perispirits, which after discarnation took on their present form. The only difference between them and other cases of zoanthropy is that normally it is individual; however, because they were a ruthless group that worked together, the phenomenon enveloped all of them, molding them to the wolf-like form, making them audacious, imprinting them with *alimentary needs* typical of the genus *canis lupus*, and keeping their minds dull... Due to automatism, they will remain in the fury of imbalance until God's mercy sends them back in excruciating reincarnations of expiation.

"The mind is always the generator of blessings or misfortunes, for aspirations of one kind or another always stem from it. When humans finally consider the power of thought that comes from their innermost being there will be radical change of moral and social behavior, making way for the important achievements of triumphant immortality.

"But for now, the process is, of course, still in the preparatory phase. It still yields to aberrations that are materialized in the physical world, characterizing the decline of ethical and moral values. The hopes of bliss capsize on the rough seas of the passions.

"On the earth, in the field of communications, there are many praised *multipliers of opinion* in tune with bestial entities that subject them to the will of their aberrations during lengthy out-of-body experiences during physiological sleep, deeply imprinting their innermost being with debauchery, delirium and moral degradation. Upon returning to the somatic body, they recall the depraved experiences they enjoyed and they encourage their admirers to pursue lust, sex laced with hallucinogenic drugs, alcohol, and pharmaceutical stimulants.

"It's no wonder the new generation indulges in loud music of immoral content at dance clubs conducive to primitivism and sensuality, where the perversion of sentiments is the tonic, and where the stimulus to violence, rebellion and aggression comprises the panorama of rebelliousness — but against what, really? They make themselves opponents of the so-called establishment, instead of developing meaningful ways to improve it, and they immerse themselves deeply in the vilest passions, making the days ahead worse for themselves and others... Consequently they get addicted to drugs and exhaust themselves with sensual, perverse pleasures.

"Still far from being properly appreciated, responsibility and duty provide a minor contribution. This liberating task will depend on the education of new generations so that new habits of sociability and healthy communication may be established, giving rise to the development of the living forces of the Good innate in all individuals.

"The scenes we see here are the result of this arbitrary and misguided behavior in space and time, transformed into suffering in the long run, but which love will modify at the right time."

There was no opportunity for further clarification and digressions on that important topic, because it began to *rain* a caustic energy reminiscent of lightning, increasing the pain of the victims torn from their bodies as a result of the en masse discarnations.

Interestingly, there was actual lightning in the dreadful darkness. These flashes were psychic in nature and had predominated in the region even before the terrible event.

Tourists from many European countries – especially Scandinavians – in addition to Americans, French and Germans, had always chosen the region for the pleasures of the body without any appreciation for the beauty of the landscapes of the South Seas with their still semi-preserved environment... Many traveled to those havens, including Thailand, the Maldives, the Phi Phi islands and others to enjoy the moral and sexual laxity of young teens sold by irresponsible parents into the trade of licentiousness... The still-effective ancestral customs of total disregard for women and other human beings facilitated widespread prostitution of girls and boys who would be abused by Westerners that could buy them very cheaply.

Over the past few years, minds had generated that unhealthy psychosphere in the areas now affected by the disaster, which actually had a purifying function for the entire region by changing customs and proposing new moral behaviors because of the suffering, and at the same time warning about the fragility and temporariness of organic life, which, unfortunately, was not yet showing any sign of improvement. On the contrary, there was revolt, bribery, diverted international aid, and the domination of the strong over the weak, who were at the mercy of their own luck as far as their bleak future was concerned.

Since religions were slowly losing prestige, holding on to rules of behavior in theory and joining forces with the unworthy temporal powers, people were without guidance, wandering around, doing what was most pleasurable and least laborious... Easy money was all that mattered so that they could get out of their poverty and imbibe the devastating consumerism.

How much Jesus' presence is missed in the world, as well as that of His ambassadors, who, over time, came to prepare His coming!

His proposals, rich with tenderness and hope, consolation and love, have not yet penetrated even His followers, let alone those who do not know Him at all, giving rise to the follies of immediacy, of emotional and moral decay in the games of unbridled desire. Spiritual enlightenment is an enormous undertaking that requires selflessness and devotion, and is compensated through the peace it provides and the joy of living without extravagance or unhealthy dependencies.

Engaged in the special activity of helping afflicted brothers and sisters, we watched a string of scenes of suffering, each one specific because each person is unique and special, his or her problems and ambitions very characteristic for his or her level of evolution.

Abdul, enveloped in soft light, could be perceived by most of the wicked spirits who were fighting over human carcasses and trying to subject their former physical hosts. He continued reciting the Koran, pleading for Heaven to help the suffering and their tormentors.

Suddenly, in the circle of woes, we saw a haggard woman who was looking for her mother, also victim of the disaster. Already voiceless, she was calling out her mother's name while trying unsuccessfully to rid herself of her own body, immediately arousing our compassion.

I approached her, patient and compassionate, and could read in her mind her drama and immense suffering.

She had been attending to her sick, elderly mother when the tidal wave tore their home off its foundation, pushing it along with coconut palms and other large trees, smashing everything in front of it.

The death of both was immediate, and she soon awoke in agony amid the ruins of what had been the place where she used to live. She had not realized her situation because, for her, the day had not dawned. Everything was still covered in the darkness resulting from the heavy environmental vibrations as she surrendered to despair in search of the elderly woman.

Strongly connected to her body, she was trying unsuccessfully to leave the place in increasing desperation.

At that moment something beautiful happened. In the dense darkness her discarnate mother emerged, led by a noble discarnate friend who was helping her approach her crazed daughter. Seeing our work of assistance and informed by her spirit mentor, she smiled and tried to thank us without words. Then she embraced her completely unbalanced daughter and started singing a sweet melody that spoke of hope, joy and reunion. The young woman gradually calmed down and fell asleep in her mother's lap.

We helped free her from her physical remains, whose last energies were absorbed by her spirit as she rested in her mother's lap.

The sweet vibrations of the woman and her distinguished spiritual stature radiated outward, touching the perispirit of her daughter, who was taken to a sphere different from ours.

The work continued without break.

Although the sun had blessed the immense area with dawn, dense darkness and unnamed afflictions continued on our side, awaiting the sublime contribution of spiritual illumination.

7
Love as Divine Power

We had continued our activities for nearly twenty hours straight and were preparing to return to our spirit community for a brief rest.

Abdul stopped his prayerful chanting and entered into deep meditation, allowing him to radiate diaphanous energies that slowly diluted the dense darkness dimly lit by Anna's torch.

Suddenly we were approached by a group of aggressive spirits organized like a band of thugs. One of them, who seemed to be the leader, roared:

"Who's responsible for the invasion of this area?"

Dr. White approached quietly and explained that he was the one responsible for the work of attending to distressed discarnates, accompanied by friends who assisted him.

He explained that there had been no invasion in that this was a *no man's land*, hit by the collective tragedy.

He was unable to continue because the arrogant spirit, dressed in the manner typical of big city gangs in the region, cut him off:

"This area belonged to me long before what you refer to as a tragedy. One of the subordinates whom I pay to keep me informed about events that might interest me said that he had been run off by foreign invaders that had taken possession of our territory.

"He asked me to come in person with my servants to resolve the matter. So here I am, demanding that you stop right now. You weren't invited."

The doctor calmly said that he was there in answer to the appeal of the country's spirit guides. They had resorted to the help of all who wanted to offer it from both planes of life, in order to reduce the afflictions caused by the tragedy.

He explained:

"Their appeal came to our community – as it had to many others – by means of the sound of a horn playing the song *Silence*, expressing the suffering that had befallen thousands of lives on the terrestrial planet... We presented ourselves to our governor and were authorized to participate in an agape of solidarity with our suffering brothers and sisters here..."

"Well," the other brashly interrupted him again, "that does not justify you or other foreigners sticking your noses in our business in disregard for our habits and customs. Ever since the time of the Dutch colonization by the East India Company in the 16th century, we nationals have rebelled against invaders of our lands... East Timor, dominated by the Portuguese centuries ago, is still a thorn in our side... Death didn't put an end to our libertarian ideals, and although we have been returning to our beloved soil through physical rebirth, we are turning to our origins in order to defend our right to construct our nationality with our own sentiments.

"We will continue to liberate our people victimized by foreign interference, whatever it costs. Not too long ago, governments worse and wickeder than ours handed us over to the West. Japan played a major role in it, generating more unhappiness and illicitly enriching its leaders, such as the one who used to be in power, as well as his predecessor, who viciously beat him without any consideration for our national ideals.

"Therefore we Indonesians have the right to apply justice using our own disciplinary and punitive methods on those who are expelled from the body by death."

"I understand your patriotic stance," Dr. White replied. "However, the boundaries you mentioned apply to earth's geography and not this realm, because everything here is divine property.

"Listening to you, one might get the impression that you are a benefactor of the suffering people, when in fact you are an unrepentant exploiter of the energies of deserters who fall into your evil traps, and who are then dragged to places of profound suffering far from any hope and mercy. Is that justice, discipline? How dare you take the dagger of true justice into your own hands when you have not yet mastered the wild impulses of your sick nature!

"We are here at the invitation of the real governors of the country, who are, therefore, the reputable ambassadors of God. Our objective is to unshackle unfortunate brothers and sisters from their remains and free them from *vampires* from the Beyond. You can be sure that we will not shirk our commitments, and that we are in no way afraid of your threats or your fearsome gang."

The thug expressed the hatred dominating him, ranting:

"That's our job and we use our own methods according to the laws in force here. We don't need any help from violators of others' rights. We can throw you out in a matter of minutes."

With a wild expression, holding a ferocious mastiff and applauded by the crazed gang, who played drums and made strange sounds with perforated tubes, he rasped:

"Now stop what you're doing, end your blabber, and get out. Leave our patients to us. We've always managed because we know how to take care of them all."

He laughed sardonically, deliriously.

Completely unperturbed, Dr. White faced him, explaining:

"My dear friend, you are completely mistaken about us because we are not at all afraid of you, nor will we do as you say. We will continue our fraternal task and would be very grateful if you and your group would just leave, and if those who wish to stay would assist us in our endeavor."

The tormenter sneered cynically and ordered:

"Attack! Wipe out these imposters and thieves!"

As if waiting for this reaction, the doctor concentrated deeply before the aggressors in that dreadful barren land, transforming himself into a blazing light that stopped the horde, who had raised their instruments of war – arrows, javelins, spears and other exotic-looking weapons – dead it their tracks.

Taken by surprise, they heard his deep, melodic, energetic and powerful voice in their own dialect:

"Repent and bow down to the will of the Lord of the Worlds.

"There comes a time in your madness that offers only one choice: forsake your hatred and wretched persecution and embrace love.

"The years have slipped away and you have remained hostile to the Good and the Truth.

"Your wickedness overflows, and instead of inspiring fear or hate, your insanity prompts compassion.

"Decades have passed since you gave way to the madness you have cultivated in the schemes of wickedness that has made your people unhappy, transferring it to the Beyond, where you have remained murderers of your own, equally miserable people, safe from your cruelty and madness.

"Listen to me! I am the voice of your conscience. It has been nullified by desperation, and has lost the use of reason, but it needs to be liberated.

"Now is your moment of joy and emancipation.

"Silence the hatred in your hearts; leave the fear of the wretches who intimidate you and join our ranks, those of the Good."

While the firm, kindly voice penetrated the acoustics of their souls, we saw showers of light falling on the swamp, rays no longer destructive as before, but which, upon touching those rebels, penetrated them, causing inner changes, and making them weep and wail.

"Free yourselves from evil," continued the instrument of Truth, "and begin loving yourselves to start with so that you may love your neighbor and, finally, God. Like us, you are children of the same Benevolent Father who compassionately awaits you. This is your moment of renewal; take advantage of it with determination and courage to break the shackles of the ignorance and perversity that have made you so miserable for so long."

When he finished, in a lofty psychic and emotional climate, the wretches threw their weapons to the ground, and overcome by the power of love, they asked for support and membership in our group. They crossed to our side and were suddenly enveloped by the soft radiance from the Messenger of the Light.

Cursing, the leader of the group ordered the dogs to be released against the deserters and us, or that we be shot with darts and arrows. But it was no use at this point because the flight was general.

As they changed sides, throwing themselves into our welcoming arms, the defensive vibratory band grew, protecting us from any kind of external aggression.

"Come also, you, who are thirsty for light and love," Dr. White said to the stunned leader.

However, with a face filled with horror, the unfortunate commander let out a strange noise, and with a weird grimace after shaking like a leaf, he was taken by something like an epileptic seizure. He screamed and literally fell to the ground.

Some of his subordinates, who were holding the dogs and instruments of war, were dismayed at what had happened and disbanded in a noisy run, screaming desperately.

Soon after, there was silence, interrupted only by the tide of convulsive sobbing of the candidates for renewal.

Gently, the Guide resumed his earlier stance and said lightheartedly:

"Jesus always wins!

"We have plenty of work ahead. Taking our frightened brothers to the proper community for shelter is our duty.

"I will enlist the assistance of other groups in the area specializing in this type of assistance.

"Love is a divine power that always triumphs!"

8
Unexpected Assistance

The unexpected incident amazed us, but not our mentor, due to his wonderful premonitory ability.

Invested with a task of such magnitude, he was revealing himself to our group only little by little.

The information about the request by the Guides of Indonesia for spiritual assistance to communities in the Beyond also resounded within us in an enjoyable and illuminating way. Since there really is no such thing as chance, all spiritually constructive labors are pre-arranged, studied carefully, and the possibilities of success or failure examined. And when they are begun, the plan moves forward surely and with well-defined goals.

Actually, I remembered when the trumpets sounded in our colony on that morning of December 26. We all gathered in prayer because our communications department immediately informed us about the great tragedy so that we could follow the tragic events. However, I had been unaware of the measures established by the Mentors and their request for assistance in the spirit world.

Moved by the divine wisdom and exchange that exists everywhere in the name of universal solidarity, I began to observe the afflicted spirits who had opted for the wise words of Dr. White, eager for their self-renewal, and now dependent on the efforts of our group.

Dr. White had been making arrangements with organizations that specialized in helping those who had repented, marked by serious mental and emotional illnesses. Their *bodies* denoted the pain experienced due to continuous years of dreadful suffering and dependence on tormenters who abused them, reducing them to slaves of their passions.

Now that their mental attitude had started to change, they began to realize the deplorable state they were in, experiencing the implacable pain of the infirmities that had ended their physical existence, as well as the deep marks of the disorders caused by the insanity they had allowed to develop ... Moreover, due to their unfortunate behavior, each one's perispirit displayed his or her previous spiteful sentiments, now exteriorized as putrid sores, deformities and amputations, and enveloped in dark, low-level vibrations.

As I looked at them with mercy and tenderness, I realized how we are all the result of what we nurture mentally.

Gathered together in a special group in order not to be mixed in with others that were awakening from the torpor of discarnation, some wept, others were still dazed, and many others appeared deranged, forming a host of wretched beings that wallowed around in unspeakable, mortifying afflictions.

A few questions about Dr. White's dialogue with the legion of aggressive spirits danced around in my mind.

At the first opportunity, I asked him:

"Having in mind the fact that the brothers who assaulted us spoke the national language and could not understand another, how were you able to communicate with them?"

The dear friend explained:

"I utilized mental waves without verbalization in words. Under the circumstances and the thought that developed the waves, those afflicted brothers *heard* in their own language because we were vibrating on the same track of thought. On the other hand, the members of our group *heard* the dialogue in the language with which we communicate with one another. Since our group is composed of spirits from different countries, our communication is mental, without the need for oral expression formulated in the patterns of each language.

"The language of the universe is thought, which modulates expressions according to the reception of each listener. The task of interpreting language belongs to the perispirit, which has stored the idiomatic matrices of the countries we have lived in during our many corporeal lives. Even when we meet those from regions where we have never reincarnated, their mind captures and decodes the thought waves. Everything happens automatically and naturally, without effort. Even so, when there is an attunement of ideas, interests or desires, the phenomenon becomes more efficient and quicker.

"During my discussion with the leader of the rebel flock, I used formulations of the English language, which were heard in Indonesian, Portuguese and Tagalog, and also by our collaborators, depending on their country of origin."

After a brief pause, he concluded:

"Imagine a symphonic orchestration that reaches our ears accompanied by a choir singing in a particular language, and we will see that we register the music and the voices, grasping their content but without understanding the words.

What is important is the melody and the emotion it awakens in us, the joy that permeates us, and the immense well-being arising from its musical effect."

The timing did not allow for our dialogue to continue. At that moment a vehicle stopped some distance away, and some workers of the Good got out and introduced themselves to Dr. White.

It was the assistance requested by those responsible for receiving and caring for the repentant brothers that had opted for renewal and understanding.

Several of these workers of charity entered our field of relief and began to assist the sufferers, leading them one by one to the vehicle hovering in the air about a meter above the ground. Some moved with difficulty, despite the assistance, but a total of eighty were soon in their seats.

The driver thanked Dr. White and the vehicle immediately sped off on its pre-established route.

I felt edified before the divine mercy that shines on all those who want to receive it.

Next to me, my friend Ivon Costa pondered the divine wisdom and the presence of love vibrating everywhere as its most beautiful manifestation.

Less than two hours before, those brothers had belonged to the lower-order spirit world, fighting against the sovereign, divine laws, albeit subjected to them. Now they were heading toward the happiness they had spurned for decades of madness and ignorance.

Meanwhile, the brothers and sisters newly awakened by our activity were in the adjacent area, sitting on a lush lawn enjoying the tenuous light of day, despite the darkness reigning nearby.

They were about to be transferred to the relief colony thanks to the selfless assistance of numerous Polynesian helpers, some having come from far-off, more primitive islands. Generous and naive, they devoted themselves with child-like joy to assisting our victimized brothers and sisters, singing some sentimental songs from the lands they inhabited before discarnating... Dressed with simplicity and wearing colorful hats, their clothes gave them a unique and harmonious beauty.

There were still minor tremors in the depths of the Indian Ocean, although there was no further damage at the surface.

Dr. White asked us to return to our headquarters for a while, and our entire group volitated to the busy community. Rather than a resting place, it resembled a huge, open-air hospital with a number of wards for the most distressed patients. The atmospheric vibrations were beneficial, providing emotional renewal for us after the natural exhaustion caused by the plane we had been laboring on.

We immediately headed for the lodgings reserved for us, and after recommending four hours of reinvigoration, prayer and reflection, our benefactor released us.

I felt moved by the harvest of mercy bestowed upon me.

While toiling on the earth, embracing the Spiritist Doctrine, I would try unsuccessfully to understand what life was like outside the fleshly garment. No matter how much my imagination looked for parameters to help me understand, everything I had managed to conceive was very pale in relation to the reality in which I now found myself.

It is very difficult to be immersed in the world of effects, trying to understand the causes, as happens with content of any kind when we try to imagine what the land awaiting us will actually be like...

The only finding is that life, motion and activity are everywhere, and that the earth is but a poor copy of that wonderful, pulsating, permanent world where we originated.

I prayed for the brothers and sisters undergoing renewal, those who had rebelled against the divine codes and now found themselves back as defeated castaways, but surviving nonetheless... At the same time, I remembered others, those whose minds and behavior kept them bound to their physical body destroyed by death, desirous of restoring its functions, tumbling into states of madness and discouragement.

Gentle peace set in and carried me off through sleep, providing me a happy dream in a place of almost unimaginable beauty.

Everything there was sound and harmony. The breeze blowing through the trees, the flowers blooming while emitting a unique tune, the most diverse expressions of nature in a festival of sound, birds of unmatched plumage, and infinitely blue skies, as if the dome were a grandiose hall in which thousands of luminous beings moved about in orderly and almost magical activity – I was thrilled by all of it...

Automatically, I accompanied a small group going to an ultramodern building made of a transparent substance, much like those in today's large cities, but more delicate. We went into a room that looked like a gothic temple, where a religious ceremony was underway. Devoid of any symbolism, the bare nave was decorated with colorful, sonorous vibrations that filtered through huge stained glass windows, giving the place a special, unique beauty.

The people gathered there were filled with joy. We began listening to a beautiful angelic being speaking about universal solidarity.

Listening to him in rapture, the musicality of his voice penetrated my spirit more through emotion than articulated words, which sounded to me like a symphony.

It would be very difficult to translate everything he expounded, because the objective was to interject the audience with sentiments of profound love, rather than expressions mixed in with the ambient music.

I was completely bedazzled as I gently returned, waking up and maintaining the incomparable impressions of those moments of rapture in some blissful place that I could not otherwise access because I did not yet deserve it.

Day broke in our community, and with my heart beating with happiness, I went in search of my friends for the new tasks ahead.

9
Existential Challenges

Although our community was able to enjoy the sun's brightness, a dark heaviness hovered over the vast, desolate area due to the collective anguish, the despair that assailed the survivors, the rebelliousness that gripped many, and, lastly, the mental disorders caused by those who had discarnated violently.

We could see the vibratory storms that produced threatening lightning above the huge, nearly black curtain covering the spiritual landscape. The condensation of morbid energies in the area was similar to what happens in the earth's atmosphere when the clash of temperatures triggers storms and tornadoes.

This psychosphere was obviously disturbing the afflicted survivors, who added even more to the formation of the dark and threatening *cumulus*.

It became a vicious circle: minds emitting gloomy waves and absorbing the harmful effects that hovered in the air...

Tenderness and compassion gripped me and I let myself be led by the blandishments of prayer for that tormented society.

The time had come for us to return to our work. We were all in good spirits from the joy that derives from the fraternal service of love, and we volitated under the command of our benefactor, as we had done when we had arrived there.

Upon reaching our destination, we immediately began our spiritual care for our suffering brothers and sisters.

My attention was called to a female spirit who was under the terrible domination of a male spirit with a dreadful appearance, psychically exploiting her in a cruel manner.

Crazed and trapped in her body, the tormented female was struggling amid the sensations of the advanced decomposition of her body and the painful obsession to which she was submitted. We could see the tormenter who was exploiting her emotionally, leading her to continuous fits of shouting, swearing and madness.

While I was contemplating her trapped in her body, which she was attempting to raise, perhaps in hopes of fleeing her plight, a discarnate tearful and distressed elderly woman approached us and informed us that she was the woman's mother.

She immediately made a composite biographical sketch of her daughter.

"My daughter," she began in tears of resignation and a feeble voice, "was a *seller of illusions*. She became a "professional" at fourteen years of age, when she was married, according to our custom, to a much older man with a respectable appearance but a vile character. The wedding was elaborate and joyful, but after two months, he sent her to an expensive brothel that he owned, where inexperienced and dreamy girls sold their bodies for the pleasures of the flesh."

She paused, wiping her tears, and continued:

"My little girl was basically forced into carnal exploitation... She received proper training for that line of business. She underwent surgery in order to prevent pregnancy, and was taught a very particular kind of seductive dance.

"Over the days and months she became as famous as she was cynical and scornful, attracting sex addicts to the place. With the natural decline, resulting from abuse and the need to sell herself more and more, she slipped into aberrant sexual behaviors and began using dangerous drugs.

"We are strict Muslims and her father died in disgust shortly after the derangement of her behavior. Out of love, I visited her more than once, warning her incessantly that what she was doing was against our religious principles, but she wouldn't show me the least bit of consideration or respect. Finally, appearing tired of my advice, in a moment of complete imbalance she kicked me out of her brothel of lust, always manipulated by her accursed exploiter – her own husband!

"My daughter had gone mad with a disease I could not comprehend. From one moment to the next, she would become violent and aggressive, dangerous and evil. She took pleasure in terrifying the servants and even some of the clients, who lamented her frequent changes of personality, which disconcerted them in their vile association with her.

"No one knew what was happening. She began to lose weight, to languish as if her energies were being sucked out of her by a strange and malevolent force.

"For me, the moral pain was too much for my fragile strength. I couldn't handle the continuous anguish as a result of my immense love for her and I died of a heart attack."

She paused and looked sadly at the beloved spirit, still victimized by her tormenter...

"Please, help her," she begged with folded hands, almost falling on her knees if we had not stopped her.

"A demonic being took possession of her and has disgraced her ever since those not so long ago days of aberration."

There was no doubt that the young dancer had attracted a terrible lover from a previous existence, one that had been psychically connected to her while she was in the physical body. Jealous of her loose conduct, he began exploiting her in her sexual perversions, usurping her emotional energies and frequently causing her to have terrible obsessive fits.

I examined the obsessor's psyche and perceived mental scenes involving the most shocking aberrations, along with his revolt due to her death caused by the tsunami, which threatened his exploitation of her energies. So deep were the links between them – perispirit to perispirit – that he stuck to her like a mollusk to its shell, perversely threatening her.

I approached the poor woman and applied soothing, calming energies, putting her in a slight torpor. Meanwhile, her mother prayed sutras from the Koran, filled with emotion while watching me apply the therapy.

Once I was able to make the spirit sleep, I began disconnecting it from its organic viscera with the help and kindness of Abdul. The two closely-linked entities reminded me of conjoined spiritual twins. The evildoer shouted deliriously, afraid of losing the prey he had exploited for years, while Abdul spoke with him kindly but forcefully about the crime he was perpetrating, informing him that his exploitation ended with her death, which had effectively separated them. Now he would have to face the adverse consequences of his cruelty.

The proper procedure was to put him to sleep too in order to provide liberating measures at a time when she would be able to contribute with renewed thoughts and sentiments. Their attraction had been the result of her behavior, which in turn had facilitated the perfect identification between the *plug* in her crown and sexual chakras and the *outlets* in her aggressor.

The Divine Laws would never resort to the means of retaliation common to human beings, who delight in rendering justice using their own unfortunate conceptions.

No one is on a position to redeem moral and spiritual debts by making themselves victims. That is just never the case, because if true, it would be a lamentable failure of the codes of divine justice.

The mechanisms of reparation are part of the higher laws of life, and they never fail. Nonetheless, the pride and intemperance of those who feel they have been harmed transform them into vigilantes, caught in powerful webs of crimes unknown to society, but which they will always have to face.

When the mother realized that her daughter was sleeping in relative peace, except for a few natural jerky movements as the unavoidable result of the mental constructions stored in her unconscious and the morbific emanations of her opponent, she smiled happily and hugged her.

For me, this was a very special case. It was the first time I was witnessing an instance of obsession that had begun during life and continued after death, with no change on the part of the merciless persecutor. During these unfortunate occurrences, the tormenter would also suffer the contingencies experienced by his victim during the process of discarnation. Exploited by the avenger, she was unconsciously intoxicating him with the emanations of her despair and loss of vital (animal) tonus from the physical body, which was absorbed by her foe.

Considering the specificity of the situation, Abdul provided a stretcher and co-workers to carry both spirits to the appropriate place for each of them.

Thrilled with happiness, the mother expressed her gratitude by unexpectedly kissing our hands, greatly embarrassing us because we were the ones who actually benefited the most.

Obsession always presents surprising aspects because of the mental and spiritual organizations that vary from individual to individual.

Observing this perturbing phenomenon always makes us ponder the inner behavior of the human being, always proceeding from the mental field, radiating in all directions and tuning in to other, compatible fields and vibratory areas that provide connections by affinity.

When people finally grasp the fact that they are responsible for everything that concerns them, individual and collective behaviors will certainly change. They will choose what leads to harmony and happiness – even if it takes a lot of effort – rather than the exhausting pleasure of one moment with its disturbing, long-term consequences. In their organic illusion, however, they prefer the intoxication of unhealthy, irresponsible enjoyment to the point of exhaustion, holding on to absurd ideas of finding miraculous solutions when the inevitable, afflicting consequences manifest.

It is not surprising that a large number turn to Spiritism and mediumship, looking for a miracle cure for the problems they created and want resolved, but perhaps without making a selfless contribution.

Existence in the physical body is a learning opportunity that life grants the spirit for its inner growth, providing it with the appropriate resources so that the *divine spark* existing in everyone may reach its fullness. Depending on how individuals behave, they will be sowing the events of their futures, which they will have to face in order to recompose themselves and fix what was damaged.

Each reincarnation is a sublime, divine concession for the blissful construction of personal immortality.

A blessed school, the earth is a beautiful haven in which we all grow spiritually, removing the heavy gangue of primitivism that impedes the brightness of the stellar diamond of the spirit that we are. The blows received during the evolutionary process are meant to liberate us, enabling the facets chiseled by pain and polished by love to reflect our spirit's sidereal beauty.

From where we were standing, we could observe the differences in conduct amongst the afflicted, identifying a greater amount of either despair or balance, which enabled us to assist them with greater or lesser effectiveness. However not all whom we sought to help could be liberated, so strong were the bonds of the sensuality of organic life, far from any kind of belief in the survival of the spirit after death.

It was not possible to digress any longer. Dr. White called us back to work, because new discarnations and assaults by animalized spirits continued.

The sight of the post-mortem occurrences surprises even those who, like us, have been in the spirit world for several years.

Physical life disguises the appearance of the spirit, which skillfully puts on a mask to show what it would like to be, without striving for its inner transformation for the better. However, the reality that characterizes it demystifies it during the process of discarnation, showing what each spirit is as well as its potential for recovery and rebalancing.

Thus the landscapes close to the border of the grave are usually filled with affliction, except those that welcome spirits who strove to live by the standards of duty regarding their neighbors and life, even without any religious affiliation. What matters is how one lived and not the beliefs one espoused. Nonetheless, religion, when freed of ignorance and devoid of fantasies and superstitions, and characterized by logic and reason, is a sublime means for accessing complete freedom. It provides lucidity and enlightenment, assisting the spirit traveler to make the best contribution to the success of its immortal journey.

There was no time for a broader discussion, and we joyfully got back to work.

10
Lessons of High Magnitude

Our work required effort and selflessness because the more we assisted suffering spirits, the more others arrived, as bodies kept washing up on the beaches, or as a result of the discarnation of traumatized individuals that had lost consciousness, and who, because they had not received assistance, had not survived their injuries, the withering away of their energies, malnutrition, or infections...

Anna continued holding the torch of luminous fluids to light up the spiritual night while at the same time contributing her invaluable help.

Father Marcus was speaking to a small group of Catholic Christians, who were still attached to their material remains.

His voice was sweet and gentle as he informed them that death should not be seen as a big disgrace...

"Everyone, when born, is marked to die," he said, "because that is the cycle of life. The opposite of life is not death, but rebirth.

"Jesus died in order that He might rise on the third day, demonstrating immortality and communicating with His beloved friends who would be left behind, awaiting the confirmation of His luminous words.

"Thanks to His return, the Gospel was confirmed, and the message it carries became one of hope so that all those who suffer at the edge of the abyss may not yield to fear or discouragement.

"Therefore, trusting that beyond death there is a realm that awaits us all is the duty of every Christian whose doctrine is based on the certainty of the victory of life over the demise of the grave."

As he was speaking, Abdul, Ivon, Oscar and I, now accompanied by two Indonesian spirits that had offered to help us out, worked to free newly-discarnates from the strong ties to their bodies, the spurious fruits of their materialism.

Although attentive to the words of the priest, as each spirit was freed, it experienced a sort of vertigo and fell over, almost unconscious, and was immediately taken from the small circle to the transportation area.

"Happy," continued the apostle of charity, "are all we who believe in our Lord Jesus Christ as the Way, the Truth and the Life. We are bound to Him by the love that gives sustenance to our emotions. Death is life, and misfortune is a blessing, because nothing happens without His permission.

"Confront the storm of despair like His disciples did when, filled with fear in the fragile boat during the storm, they begged for His help, and He calmed the winds and waves.

"In Him we have the confident Mariner who will guide the boat of our immortality to the sublime port of peace.

"So fear not. Be confident and help us to help you.

"As frightening as physical death may seem, life is a triumph over all injunctions, and nothing can destroy it. Therefore, to leave your useless corporeal vehicle behind, thanking it for its help during the journey you have just completed, and to advance confidently on the course of immortality is cause for endless joy. You will meet, once again, the loved ones who preceded you, who have been waiting for you in order to reorganize your families through the blessed bonds of love. So rejoice and have faith, for your present suffering will soon be a chapter in your past."

Pausing for a moment so that his words could be heard and understood, he remained in prayer, which adorned him with a tenuous spiritual light emanating outward in that marsh of despair, externalizing the grandeur that characterized his level of evolution.

Taken with obvious emotion, his listeners wept and pleaded for help, touching us all.

In this climate of high vibrations of love and compassion, we could perceive the value of the sentiments of affection when interacting with the most distressed brothers and sisters. If love cannot meet the essential goals it is meant for, its purpose is utopian and vain.

There was no other reason why Jesus chose love as the noblest and most indispensable achievement to which humans can aspire.

While we rejoiced in the results of Father Marcos's convocation, we were also aware of the unfortunate results arising from the folly and delusion of individuals who are far from the knowledge of spiritual reality.

The awful phenomena of lycanthropy constrained us, leading us to reflection, both in relation to those who suffered the affliction, as well as to their defenseless victims, who were, after all, victims of themselves.

Ignorance of the Laws of Life immerses the spirit in the most abysmal state of primitivism, uninterested in the ascent that would lift it above its deplorable situation.

My mind harbored no sentiment of reproach or criticism, because somehow we are all travelers in the night of dense darkness, headed for the bright and shining day.

The religious atavisms that promised them first-fruits and states of glory after biological death sustained some who were aware of what had happened as they awaited the arrival of mythological angels. However, they would soon fall into despair, blasphemy and rebelliousness, complaining about their supposed abandonment. Besides being a profoundly thoughtless attitude, this transference of responsibility for our actions to the Divine One is very convenient because it provides a totally distorted view of reality, transferring it to the world of fantasy and magic, where anything is possible...

Only when human beings truly awaken to self-consciousness and their responsibilities do they start the process of discovering truth and duty.

Until then, individuals transfer to others all that concern them, whether by blaming others, or while undergoing the requirements of evolution, hoping that *angels of mercy* work for them in a supernatural and privileged way, thus freeing them from putting forth an effort for their self-illumination.

Right after Father Marcos's peroration, Dr. White approached us, and perceiving the questions dancing around in my mind, he rescued me with some invaluable clarifications.

"My dear Philomeno," he began gently, "you know that all occurrences contribute to our growth toward God. Despite our immense respect for all religions and their necessary role, so far they have been based on magical and non-rational conduct, unfortunately. They do not hold their adherents responsible for their acts, which accounts for the consequences that always reach them, usually in a climate of distress as a result of their negative moral content.

"In presenting their special gods or prophets – some of whom suffered from behavioral disorders, blending truthful information with their own conflicts, thus giving rise to nullifying and perverse revelations – they claim to be responsible for the *word* of God, humanizing and limiting Him to their passions rather than the imperishable greatness and infinitude of the Creator, and giving those revelations the appearance of indisputable truths. More concerned with outward formulas and precepts than with the internal sentiment of devotees, they strive to attract more adherents without the least concern for qualifying them for their brief existence on earth, and consequently, their immortality after the body.

"Unable to understand the Absolute Causality of the Universe, they set forth their concepts in the poor language of their needs, seizing multitudes, who do not know how to think, playing on their unhealthy fanaticism, the heritage of spiritual primitivism, as a means for instant salvation. All it takes is a bit of human effort to earn eternal recompense or, if this is not achieved, terrible eternal punishment without the slightest possibility of receiving mercy or compassion. Nevertheless, they emphatically claim that the All-Loving Father is also All-Merciful, in an absurd paradoxical placement...

"Thus, these automata of faith stagger around in the physical world, deceived by fraudulent information, assimilated without reasoning and received as an inheritance from their ancestors, whom they think they are honoring by also following their precepts, entering the spirit world without concern for their self-enlightenment. Their dogmas, their ceremonies, all developed with cruelty, belittle humans, enslaving them in fear and imprisoning them in ignorance, making it very difficult to enlighten them during the first stages after the grave."

He paused for a moment, looked sadly at the enormous crowd of spirits afflicted by madness and unbounded despair, and continued:

"It is at this stage of suffering that the compassion of heaven sends these sufferers back to the blessed earthly school for reincarnation in severe expiation or harsh trials, enabling them to understand the laws of justice and the duties that must comprise every lifetime.

"Even if one fiercely denies the doctrine of physical rebirth, that does not keep it from being a blessed universal law of unparalleled significance, without which we would remain stuck in the initial stages of evolution, without a chance of intellectual and moral growth.

"Perfectly compatible with the law of progress, which only occurs through the process of personal experiences, reincarnation gradually enables the *inner god* to develop and grow deep within the spirit, drawing it toward God.

"As we watch the bitter pain that dominates these thousands of spirits, mistaken in their beliefs about the Abundant Life, in their fixations about transitory things as if they were permanent, once again we realize that we, earthly individuals accustomed to the vagaries of selfishness, are still stuck in spiritual infancy and lack the sublime enjoyments of solidarity and love.

"Religion tells us that the grave does not mean annihilation; hence we know that life goes on. It would be logical therefore to live in a manner consistent with that belief, but that is not the case. Disputes and material fixations control our inner world in such a way that, consciously or not, we indefinitely postpone the moment of departure from the body. When we are young, we long for it to occur in old age, and when old age settles in and we sense the approach of discarnation, fear assails us, leading quite a few of us into depressive disorders, rebelliousness or some other type of imbalance.

"It would take only a few moments of daily reflection about the transience of physical life to prepare ourselves to joyfully wait for the moment of discarnation. What prisoner does not yearn for freedom, and who, at seeing a fellow cellmate set free, does not also long for that great moment? And with what joy he greets it when it arrives!

"The metaphor explains very well how we should behave, but unfortunately, that does not happen.

"A not too far off day, however, will come when religions will be access doors to life and not the prison of ignorance and absurdity. Thus let us remember that all the prophets and founders of religions, however lofty and noble they may have been, cannot be equated to Jesus Christ, who sent them to earth so that they would weaken the shadows of cruelty a little in order that He could establish the beacons of the *Kingdom of Heaven* in the world. Even those who came after His advent have been ministers of His kingdom. Hence the Comforter He promised has come to hurry those days of true communion between Creator and creatures.

"Therefore let us not get discouraged; let us fulfill our duty."

I found myself amazed and edified, wondering how the noble doctor had come to these conclusions, knowing that he had been of the Anglican persuasion in his previous existence.

Perceiving my thoughts, the benevolent friend smiled and concluded:

"My dear Philomeno, knowledge travels from here to the earth, not from there to here... Thus, participating in study groups in our community, I learned about the Spiritist Revelation and its greatness for human beings. That is why I am engaged in the task of our group."

And because more questions assailed my mind, still good-humored and wise he interrupted me:

"The endeavor awaits us. You will find your answers as you work with Jesus for the good."

11
Continued Learning

Steeped in the dense psychosphere of human afflictions, the region in which we operated remained terrifying. Although the day was shining with light and the sky was a cloudless turquoise-blue from the brightness of the sun, the presence of the colossal tragedy overshadowed the rubble-strewn landscape.

It looked like a war zone that had suffered heavy artillery along with destruction by air strikes.

Near the immense, once paradisiacal beach, shattered trees bobbed on the gentle waves. Others had piled up on the sand and in the vast region hit by the tsunami's fury of destruction...

People wandered aimlessly around the piles of rubble, trying to find the bodies of the missing...

In one of the emergency hospital tents there was a lot of activity by incarnates and discarnates.

I was observing the situation, when a discarnate woman with northern European features, reminiscent of her last earthly journey, approached Dr. White and asked for help.

She said that her grandson, a young man of twenty-five, used to visit the region frequently with friends from their country to enjoy its many perks of pleasure.

Bearer of a vile character and a user of chemical drugs, he attracted young and inexperienced local girls due to his athletic bearing and unique surfing skills...

Because of these qualities, he had become an unconscionable philanderer who took pleasure in corrupting his victims, forcing them into drug addiction and the sex trade.

He would finance the trips of certain girls interested in adventure and would market them to mafia organizations that turned them into sex slaves in his own and other countries. As soon as the duped girls arrived in the Nordic cities of Europe, their passports were confiscated and they were told they would have to pay for their trip after all and everything they would incur from then on.

Compared with most Europeans, the almost teenage girls' exotic looks fascinated the corrupted clientele, and when the girls realized their predicament, it was too late for any saving measures...

The woman had become used to his infamous conduct, but the wretch was her grandson, for whom she was asking for help.

As his grandmother, she had tried to inspire him to change his behavior, having had repeated encounters in the *dream realm*, but with no healthy outcome.

Emotional, she remained silent before the attentive benefactor and then finished:

"I have been told by benevolent spirits about the work you have been doing with your team, and although this is a private case, I am pleading for any help you might give.

"He was at Hotel X at the time of the earthquake and was carried off with the collapsed building by the giant wave. He was nearly buried in the rubble, and only now, several days later, he was found alive and driven to the emergency room of that makeshift hospital erected by foreigners."

Dr. Charles asked Oscar and me to accompany him, while the others continued with their work.

When we reached the operating room, we saw many being attended in serious condition.

After the doctors placed him on an apparatus for computerized study, they concluded that his case was extremely delicate. He was in a coma, with a large area of his brain compromised by cranial traumas received when the building collapsed and the wall of water hit him.

Dr. White observed him and explained to the grandmother:

"The young man is critical and there is no possibility of recovery. The number of days he went without assistance has compromised his other organs and his heart has become highly disrupted under the exhausting effort. It has stopped twice, which has in turn compromised the brain even more because of the anoxia...

"But worse yet is his spiritual condition."

We saw his spirit still attached to its body, thrashing around in the powerful grip of two cruel adversaries who were caning him. Their hatred was being absorbed by the victim, especially through the brain, heart and solar chakras, affecting his weakened heart.

One of them, whose face was a demonic mask, threatened him:

"You're going to die, you wretch! We want you here as soon as possible to punish you for the evil you did to our daughters. How could you ruin them in the sex trade by using their ignorance for your insatiable pleasures in your moral sickness? We shall never forgive you for invading our homes and disgracing our loved ones. If there is divine justice, we will be its intermediaries and will apply it according to what you did to your victims."

Uproarious, mad laughter accompanied each accusation.

The other also shouted at the accused:

"Damned foreigner, wretched vulture who's degraded everyone who passes by your road of miseries! Because we're poor, you cynically think you can corrupt our girls and haul them off into slavery in your land? You're going to pay for your crimes in ways you could never even imagine since we have powers that you don't, you miserable wretch!"

An ongoing string of reproaches was voiced between grinding teeth and aggressive hands.

Others also made accusatory complaints, surrounding the poor wretch with their angry faces, causing him infinite dread and leading him to struggle in tears and continuous fainting spells.

Astounded, I looked at Dr. White, who explained:

"Our brothers are trying to kill him, that is, they are trying to wrest control of his body by poisoning his heart with vibrations of hatred until it stops beating... In its present state of weakness, it cannot handle the ingestion of poisonous fluids emitted by his enemies much longer. In addition to the other causes of imbalance, they are making his condition even worse."

After a bit of thought, he emphasized:

"Yet he has to make it."

He gave no further explanation, but added:

"Unless he regains his lucidity, he will have a long vegetative life of reparation."

He immediately approached the litigants, condensing his perispirit so they could see him, and then serenely began speaking with them.

"I acknowledge," he began with a kindly tone of voice, "the validity of your arguments regarding the patient. However, the application of justice is up to God, who knows each of us in depth. We can never know how to correct someone when dominated by hatred and desirous of revenge... There's no doubt that this young man is reckless and has been committing heinous crimes. But snatching him away by death would be a perverse, unjustified crime, because evil must in no way be part of the context of life!

"So, considering the circumstances, trying to kill him violates the Sovereign Laws, for nobody has the right to take the club of justice into their own hands."

Furious, they retorted, while others, agitated, began shouting, trying to create a disturbance:

"We don't need a foreign judge," one shot back. "We know our laws and according to them, according to the Koran, as well as to Sharia, we know what we are doing in applying lashes corresponding to the crime, and there have been many, many crimes of dishonor and degradation of lives committed by him. On the earth they are punished with death, which we will apply here too... We don't need the interference of Christians in our decisions, giving ourselves permission to continue with our purposes, because we are within the Law."

"That might seem right," responded the resolute benefactor. "But even so, the Koran also speaks of mercy, and that only Allah is just, benevolent, wise and able to forgive the worst offenders... Muhammad recognizes the greatness of Jesus and His doctrine, so truth is universal, and in the case in question, it doesn't matter if Muslims or Christians interfere, as long as it is based on sentiments of mercy and love, for both are of a divine, irrevocable character."

"We're not interested in your help. We only care about achieving our goals, and we won't change them."

"I understand your pain and everyone else's perfectly... Pain is everywhere during these turbulent times. Only divine wisdom knows the reasons for everything that has happened since the time of the earthquake... I've been really touched by the sentiment of solidarity between countries from different parts of the world, contributing to the victims of the terrible occurrence. There's been no concern about the beliefs, morals or conduct of those in distress. All are possessed of a healthy desire to help, to show love and respect for the suffering of others.

"The same attitude of solidarity applies beyond the physical forms under the auspices of Love.

"Since you are insensible to compassion, I appeal to the mercy we all need before God. Do you by any chance consider yourselves free from errors? Did you live without having contracted debts or liens concerning the painful situations of others?

"Well then, do unto the destroyer of your peace as you would like others to do unto you if you were in his place."

His words were spoken with immense compassion and tenderness, enveloping the aggressors in soothing vibrations of harmony, something that stunned them momentarily before they resumed their attack.

"I have offered you the blessing of charity for this criminal and you have rejected it," stated Dr. White. "Now I find myself in the position of having to appeal to other resources available in situations like this."

He began to pray in deep concentration, which we were more than willing to join.

A gentle light surrounded them, and Anna, who had been holding the torch aloft in her right hand, set it on the ground, and approaching both within the higher light, she embraced them kindly while the doctor released the spirit from the pressure of its foes.

Suddenly his two enemies were overcome by a strange stupor, and supported by the spirit nurse, they were set on the ground in order to be transferred by benevolent aids summoned mentally by Dr. White, who then applied wholesome energies to the comatose patient.

We saw his spirit *encasing* itself in its body, and soon thereafter it began to convulse.

"He's going to make it. He will receive skilled resources and will soon be able to return home, where he will undergo a long trajectory of moral recovery."

Very moved, the discarnate grandmother thanked the spirit doctor and embraced her dear grandson.

When we returned to our labors, it seemed the right time to ask:

"From what I gather, spirit adversaries were plotting his discarnation; correct?"

Always kind and attentive, the mentor replied:

"We can call such aggression an attempt at spiritual murder."

"Does that happen a lot?"

"More often than you might imagine… We must never forget that the spirit world is the realm of causes, where the actions and deeds that materialize on the earth originate. The source of sublime inspiration, it also gives rise to devastating reactions when their authors are on the lower levels of evolution. In colonies of pain and shadow, perverse minds draw up awful plans that inspire earthly wanderers, desensitizing them and assisting them in their misguided conduct.

"In psychic partnership, these heartless pursuers of the Good hypnotize those with whom they lived in the spirit realm and use them with a coldness that shocks us, coming from their devastating mental constructs.

"With the incarnate spirit held in the vibratory mesh of its rivals due to moral commitments to them, it becomes subject to their control, experiencing bitter pain that can cause organic disasters in the body. The mind is the bearer of energies that move through the physical apparatus, and when they are deleterious, they produce similar effects. In the same way that strong emotions in the waking state damage the body and cause very serious disturbances in the physiological machinery, those that take place during partial disengagement during sleep, coma or similar situations resonate in the cells, either damaging or harmonizing them, if they result from joys and blessings.

"Everything that occurs in the body comes from the psyche, and therefore from the spirit, which is the driver of the material carriage.

"Although connected to the Muslim doctrine, our brothers know the reality of life after death and they behave like countless discarnate Christians and others who may or may not believe in immortality.

"There are quite a few who perfect their pernicious behaviors before reincarnation so that they can give them expansion during the organic journey.

"The reality is the same, varying only in external forms, thus making it easy for all of us to be enveloped in its powerful manifestations.

"One more reason for immortal contents to be spread to everybody to guide them more effectively during incarnation. Knowledge of the truth is liberating because it is engraved on the thought and actions, guiding individuals during their illuminative development."

In the meantime, we arrived at our area of usual activities and continued to assist the desperate brothers and sisters whom death had surprised without notice, and who, immersed in the allure of the body, never gave themselves time to reflect on the unavoidable presence of death.

12
Life Responds as Planned

The activities continued arduously, considering the number of victims that had been swept away by the tragedy.

Unfortunately, without any preparation beforehand for confronting the spiritual reality, they were struggling in the strong bonds of their putrefying bodies, trying to reanimate them in order to recommence the Dantesque feast of illusions. When their efforts were not crowned with success – and they certainly never were – despair drove them to madness, evidence that they had lived only for the sensations.

Of course there were many spirits that had been ennobled by their labors, dignity, religious faith and moral values. These were assisted by beloved family members who had gone before them on the journey of Immortality, and by selfless mentors who had assisted them during their earthly journey...

However I am referring to the majority, the careless mass of humanity, for which life means only a trip to the land of chimeras, devoid of its profound significance.

But since God's love is always present, they never lacked effective aid from the spirit world, as was the case with our small group of servants of the Good.

Oscar was helping me assist an anguishing discarnate woman who was trying unsuccessfully to break her perispiritual bonds. I became aware of her advanced state of pregnancy, noticing the presence of the spirit-fetus, which lay sleeping after its organic death, although still magnetized to its mother's body.

Since I did not know what to do, I resorted to Dr. White, who suggested that we first try to get the mother to fall asleep in order to proceed with the *delivery*.

We both concentrated and applied calming energies to the afflicted woman, who slowly fell asleep.

Dr. White asked Anna to attend to the baby boy while he applied special resources to his *crown chakra* area, diluting the dense energy, which started to change tonality and shape until it became like a thread completely loosened from the fibers of energy that bound the two.

While he did this, the sleeping mother expelled a thick, shapeless mass, as if she had given birth to it.

We soon realized it was a mental condensation from both son and mother, accumulated in her uterus where gestation had been taking place.

From that moment on, her sleep became reparative, tranquil...

In the final step of the procedure, the spirit, who did not manage the blessing of reincarnation, experienced a great shock, as we saw the body of the discarnate woman absorb the dense fluids that had been retaining the fetus.

I noticed, curiously, that the process of decomposition immediately sped up. The bacteria responsible for destroying the tissues seemed vitalized and they increased infinitely, voraciously, something that I had not witnessed before.

Dr. White explained that the microbial flora and fauna responsible for composing and decomposing the physical apparatus are maintained by a natural law; however it is the universal fluid that either gives them vitality, or destroys them when they are no longer necessary.

In the present case, the *physical impressions* transmitted by the spirit were somehow preserving certain organic areas that were less sensitive to decomposition, slowing down their degenerative process.

The newly discarnate fetus was taken by Anna to one of the special areas, from where it would then be taken away and awakened elsewhere to live in a community of infants suitable for its future development.

The sleeping mother was led to the place where she would also be transferred along with those we could consider as improved, and who, upon awakening in the recovery area, would suffer less distress.

She had expected the little one with the infinite tenderness of someone who wanted to experience a dignified motherhood. The husband, explained Dr. White after some reflection, had also discarnated, but on one of the country's other islands, where he had been engaged in business.

Of course, due to the law of affinity he would soon wake up and have the means to reconnect with his loved ones, using the resources of guidance and clarification that were set up in our sphere of action.

I was greatly edified by these lessons.

And because I still needed some clarifications, I asked my noble friend to help me understand the disturbing incident involving the discarnation of the pregnant woman and her little son in those circumstances, considering the fact that he had almost been at the moment of rebirth in the physical body.

Dr. White thought for a moment and then explained to Oscar and me:

"During her next-to-last incarnation, our sister lived on one of the thousands of islands of Indonesia – the one where her husband discarnated this time. He had also been her husband on that former occasion.

"They indulged in the magical and superstitious practices very common throughout the region, especially on many of the remote, still culturally primitive islands... Regarded as possessing spiritual gifts, she and the unfortunate spirits with whom she was attuned demanded sacrifices of children because their innocence would bring joy, health and happiness to those who were allowed to use them. Thus they murdered a number of defenseless children, whose ignorant and wicked parents allowed their immolation, victims of barbarous customs...

"When the pair discarnated, they were captured by some of their victims, who inflicted them with severe punishment, terrible imprisonment and humiliating submissions... Debtors and their insensitive collectors are always in tune with each other.

"But since justice is always present, love came to them in the form of mercy and they both reincarnated this last time. They were forced to end it very painfully, extremely sadly.

"After their expiation, which they imposed on themselves out of illuminative necessity, they will resume, on another occasion, the process of growth toward God, and will build a home where they will be given a large family including a number of their former victims, now wretched and thirsting for revenge... Love is the light that erases the darkness of hatred, diluting it with the clarities of tenderness and understanding."

He paused for a bit and then concluded:

"The little boy, who came to her, magnetized by her perispirit after having forgiven them, repaired the evil he had inflicted on them during the time they were in the lower realms of the spirit world. He too will reincarnate, filled with hope and joy.

"The father discarnated on the same island, where he had practiced black magic and committed heinous crimes, having suffered a lengthy process before discarnating. He was slow unraveling himself from his physical shackles and experienced superlative afflictions until his body decayed completely.

"The Sovereign Laws always take charge in rebalancing order where aggression and crime, foolishness, and the crudity of sentiments have been expressed. No one who impairs life can continue in freedom, because the individual will remain drawn to error until he or she regains peace resulting from a nobly exercised duty and a harmonized conscience.

"On the other hand, wherever foolish attackers may be, their unforgiving victims will be bound to them devising plans for revenge.

"Therefore those who live in harmony, disencumbered of their moral debts, will experience the true happiness that nothing can consume."

When he finished, he left us with a sense of encouragement, marked by the joy of living the endeavor of self-enlightenment.

The night, however, continued gloomy, menacing. Somehow, lightning, thunder and intermittent rain made our work more trying since they were the result of spiritual storms rather than terrestrial phenomena, from the coarse vibrations and magnetic fields overloaded with harmful energies.

In the imagination of someone less experienced, he or she would soon have the impression of dealing with the mythological Hell, where there is no *glimmer of mercy or compassion...*

The difference is that God's love was active here, decreasing the constricting tentacles of suffering that had almost instantly reaped tens of thousands of lives in full physiological exuberance and time-consuming physical illusion.

But there was no time for further reflection – there would be another time for that. Right now we had to serve as best we could without measuring our efforts to liberate misguided brothers and sisters, regardless of their origins, the circumstances of their discarnation or the religion they professed. The Good does not stop before any type of border, limitation or prejudice, because it is a divine emanation for the edification of life.

I noticed once again that each individual is a special being, a veritable *universe* to discover, unknown to him or herself. Consequently, every discarnation is also special, typical of each individual because it is characterized by his or her own personal reality.

It is extremely difficult to establish comparative rules regarding human life and discarnation. Of course there are biotypes that serve as a pattern for drawing parallels that help with understanding the circumstances and occurrences.

Understandably, we were now faced with such diversity of behavior among those discarnates who refused to accept the phenomenon that had ended their lives and snatched them from the physical realm. Unforeseen circumstances, manifesting with titanic destructive power, had caught them completely off guard, and they had not even had time to grasp what was happening to them. The giant wave had been so swift and overwhelming that it had dragged off everything in front of it, leaving a trail of unimaginable destruction...

Collectively transferred to the spirit world without noticing one another, all were prisoners of their own shadows and allures, without any emotional structure for perceiving what had just happened, leaving them deranged...

I was still pondering the drama of the pregnant discarnate woman, when my attention was drawn to another deplorable woman strongly connected to her remains. She was screaming, inspiring compassion in us and sarcasm in a mob of perverse obsessors, who were tormenting her with vulgar jeers as she tried to break the bonds to go look for her missing son. She was more or less aware of her death, but not the forces that kept her connected to her almost totally destroyed body.

She would call for her son with a poignant voice and then enter a state of derangement, trying to pull out her hair, injuring and throwing herself to the ground over and over, seeking to raise her material wreckage.

Dr. White approached and listened to her psychically, trying to read on her mental landscape the events moments before the collective tragedy.

He told us that she had been far from the beach in her humble home when it collapsed under the power of the wave... She had discarnated immediately, crushed under the rubble.

The shock had put her to sleep for some time before she woke up in desperation less than a day later, more or less aware of what had happened.

"Her greatest anguish," he explained, "was that she didn't know what had happened to her little boy, her reason for living during the period of widowhood that had surprised her months before."

With fatherly benevolence and wisdom drawn from his noble existence, he tried to stop her for a while by enveloping her in luminous rays, limiting her movements. Then after saying a few words to his dedicated nurse, he began to converse with the desperate woman.

His powerful thought was captured in a clear manner through images decoded by the suffering spirit, and he managed to calm her down, bit by bit.

In the meantime, Anna arrived, bearing in her arms a smiling and beautiful child of little more than a year old, who had discarnated and quickly recovered from the drama. She presented him to the doctor.

He placed the jovial infant in the arms of the poor woman, making her smile and calm down enough to begin singing a lullaby to put him to sleep.

We were immediately asked to weaken the perispiritual bonds that held her to her corpse, and shortly thereafter she was completely free.

Stunned at the moment of emancipation, she seemed to lose her balance due to the surrounding gravity, but was assisted by Anna, who took the little one while we held on to the mother. Dr. White hypnotized her so that she could fall peacefully to sleep.

Stretcher bearers arrived to take her and the sleeping child to the appropriate area.

The miracles that love works are continuous and rich in beauty, overcoming the *abyss of death*.

Consequently, the time spent in that particular abyss dragged by slowly and painfully, loaded with unusual events that endeared us at one moment, afflicted us at another, but always awakened our love and compassion in all cases.

13
Making up for Lost Time

We returned to the community periodically for needed rest before continuing our relief efforts for our discarnate brothers and sisters spiritually bereft of illuminative resources.

The number of corpses exposed on beaches and in cities victimized by the collective tragedy was slowly decreasing, while the wreckage was being removed and buildings were being reconstructed.

The suffering of the survivors was appalling; nevertheless, the sublime impulse of life to overcome misfortune kept them going and helped them rebuild their lives.

The time reserved for us to accompany the workers of the Good passed quickly, and Ivon and I had to return to our own Sphere for other commitments awaiting us within the directional lines of our earlier conference with the Benefactor who had come from the Pleiades constellation.

We thanked Dr. White for all he had done to help us understand the mechanisms of the Divine Laws, and taken by emotion we said goodbye to the rest of our friends as well.

Dr. White had invited two spirits who had lived in Indonesia to replace us, since the hard work would continue for a long time.

On the day of our return, the sun enriched the region with its blessed rays and the landscape still showed the indelible marks of the devastating tsunami.

When we boarded the vehicle that would take us home, we could see, off in the distance, the vast region shrouded in dense darkness, in which lights shone from time to time, representing the workers of charity in their efforts to apply the treasures of the Good on behalf of those hungry for knowledge and personal harmony.

We had benefitted from new experiences that amazed us due to their originality, since we had never had occasion to be involved with that kind of assistance before.

I was impressed by the *miracle* of life, which breathes vitality back into the drought of summer, causes the dried branches to bud and the tender shoots to appear when spring arrives, and revives faint hearts in the uneven struggle, providing inner spiritual growth…

It triumphs in all seemingly destructive situations and points toward immortality as the supreme victory of human existence.

When we reached our community, we were greeted warmly by our old friends. Accompanying us to our homes, they asked us about our charitable endeavors among the unfortunate brothers and sisters in Indonesia…

As far as possible, we described the uplifting experiences and the lessons we had absorbed, especially the fellowship among spirits acclimated to different faiths, but united by the same sentiments of love, compassion and charity.

Indeed, we discovered the solidarity that should exist between Muslims and Jews, Catholics and Protestants, Spiritists and other believers – or even non-believers – which filled us with ineffable, inner joy as we rediscovered Divine Wisdom pulsing in everything, as well as the power of fraternal solidarity, which does not submit to the unbending whims of the passionate ego.

Spirits of different origins stopped over in our community periodically to work with us in the light of the teachings of Jesus and Allan Kardec, overcoming the dogmatic impediments of their former beliefs and adopting the universal standard, far removed from abbreviations and terminologies, but sharing the same lofty goals and liberating purposes.

Although Ivon Costa resided in another colony situated over Central Brazil, based on the beautiful mountains of Minas Gerais, I invited him to stay with us for the next few days before returning to the earth to pursue other commitments.

Understandably, the exchange between spirit colonies is constant and natural, as happens on the earth between different communities that sustain and interact with one another.

Although each has its own specific characteristics, they all operate for the moral development of their discarnate inhabitants, preparing them for future commitments in blessed reincarnations.

Since our work with Dr. Charles White was finished, we would depart within two days on a new venture. We did not yet know who our mentor would be, although we had been invited to join a new group of spirit workers.

For us, rest entails the renewal of energies for spiritually uplifting endeavors, revitalizing and helping us to better understand the lessons of life, expanding our horizons of service to others, which ultimately results in service to ourselves.

Thus it is a bit different than the kind of rest needed by incarnates, whose strength and balance are renewed according to their individual organic parameters for the commitments of evolution.

Life does not ever cease to vibrate. If it did, it would reduce everything to the chaos of the beginning...

Therefore it is necessary to act, to make up for time previously squandered on wrongful behaviors, selfishness and the constant pursuit of pleasure.

In one way or another we were waiting somewhat anxiously for details about the new program.

The success of the commitment we had just concluded stimulated us to wait for our new challenges with joy and gratitude to Heaven.

Those who think that the righteous repose after death are mistaken. Throughout the universe, only the law of action and spiritual growth reigns.

In the meantime we learned that the caravan of service to our brothers and sisters on the earth would be impressive both in quality and in quantity of members, that it would be divided into various groups working in different locations, and that it would be presided over by the learned geneticist Dr. Artemio Guimarães.

I was a little familiar with his fascinating story, which had projected him to the status of head of the reincarnation department in our colony.

The eminent spirit had discarnated about thirty years ago after a laborious life as a missionary in Brazil.

He had reincarnated with the mission of striving to make use of the mechanisms of life preservation, having dedicated his work to healthy human reproduction.

Having been reborn into a modest home in order to know hardship and overcome it early on in Rio de Janeiro, he was still very young when he started to display the superior abilities he had brought with him from the spirit world.

A friendly and vivacious, intelligent and benevolent child, he became a responsible and studious young man who helped his widowed mother, a real fighter who had agreed to receive him into her loving arms while simultaneously attending night school.

With Herculean sacrifices he overcame the vicissitudes of youth and remained true to the principles of duty, surmounting environmental, aggressive and disruptive conditions, embracing the desire to save developing fetuses and fighting boldly against every form of criminal abortion.

To better carry out his future ministry, he moved to Sao Paulo after his mother discarnated, the victim of tuberculosis from organic weakness and poor nourishment. He worked harder and harder until he managed to enter the famous university of that city, attending it with a fighting and tenacious spirit.

Identifying with the noble masters of Medicine – true apostles that have comprised the august breed of many generations of honorable scientists and professionals – he devoted himself to biology and embryology, joining a group of colleagues in the nascent field of genetic engineering.

After graduating with his medical degree, he received a merit-based scholarship to a distinguished American university and joined a closed circle of researchers studying anovulatory cycles and methods of contraception, which would contribute to the drastic reduction of the heinous crime of abortion. He threw himself fully into his research and became a highly-regarded scientist in that field, achieving with his peers a broad knowledge of human fertilization.

With the advancement of optics and technology around the manufacture of microscopes, especially electron microscopes, he was able to understand the *miracle of human fertilization*, selecting ova and sperm in experiments that would eventually lead to the grand achievement of *in vitro fertilization*, artificial insemination, enabling thousands of people to procreate...

As society became increasingly aware of the use of contraceptives, fighting against the fanaticism of certain intolerant religious segments, he became interested in the specialized studies regarding DNA and the likely future decoding of the human genome. However, he did not get the opportunity to see the completion of that extraordinary project, whose rough draft was presented to the world for the first time in June of 2000 and confirmed in April of 2003 on the fiftieth anniversary of the discovery of the DNA double helix by the scientists Drs. James Watson and Francis Crick...

He discarnated from exhaustion from severe and continuous work, the victim of cardiac arrest, which did not put an end to his bold scientific career, as he resumed it in the spirit world.

He left behind a widow – a dedicated companion and also a medical scholar in the area of infectious diseases – and two adult children.

Considered a victor in the mission he had embraced, today he is regarded among us as an estimable apostle in the area of human fertilization, a specialist in reincarnations.

It would be under the command of this eminent spirit that approximately five hundred workers would be returning to the beloved planet for the preparation of the new era, making way for mass reincarnations of migrants from one of the stars in the constellation of the Pleiades in the sublime endeavor of helping the earth reach the level of *world of regeneration.*

It is true that other teams had already preceded us; that many others would follow in different countries, and that even in the blessed lands of the Southern Cross,[6] countless hardworking servers of Jesus would carry out similar activities.

Although bearers of spiritual meaning, we were mere helpers in a highly important experience.

Those responsible for the various groups had been devising plans in our colony and in many others (since the project was international and without boundaries) for more than ten years so that blessed spirits could find skilled resources for their ministries in the coming days of the future.

Thus it was with supreme happiness that, on the night scheduled for the first contact, Ivon and I headed for the ecumenical temple – referred to earlier – where we would all meet in order to become familiar with the guidelines drawn up for the new endeavor.

At 7:30 p.m. we went into an enclosure smaller than the previous one. It reminded us of a Greek amphitheater covered with a transparent substance that allowed us to see the splendid evening with its starry chrysanthemums glittering off in the distance.

A soft melody came from the organ, filling the environment with musical harmony.

---

[6] i.e., Brazil. – I.R.

Cheerful, charming special guests – those who would participate in the unusual event – filled the auditorium.

At the appointed time, we had the immense pleasure of seeing the governor of our colony enter, accompanied by administrators from the various sectors. All were led to the head table and chairs reserved in front.

Created by selfless servants of Jesus under the auspices of Francis of Assisi, our colony houses a sizeable population of spirits who used to live in Brazil, along with a few from France who had settled in the golden-green land during their latest existences.

With a few exceptions, everyone in the auditorium had been members of the hosts of the Comforter – according to the Spiritist revelation – whereas the few others, although without knowledge of the Doctrine introduced by Allan Kardec, could, due to their activities, be regarded as Spiritists at heart within the definition of the Codifier.

The master of ceremonies was the spirit Jose Lopes Netto,[7] who was enveloped in a bright, tenuous opaline light indicating his intellectual and moral elevation.

The ceremony began with a young singer who, accompanied by the organ, sang the beautiful religious piece *Panis Angelicus*, authored by St. Thomas Aquinas for the

---

[7] Jose Lopes Netto - born in 1882, in Curitiba (PR), was the son of Genesio and Clara Lopes. On November 11, 1904 and only 22 years old, he was bestowed with the post of 2nd Secretary of the Board of the Spiritist Federation of Paraná. He discarnated at age 35, after playing a role of great importance for that organization, having served various executive positions, including that of President. A *seeing, somnambulistic, psychographic, hearing* medium, and a vibrant, exciting speaker, according to Dr. Lins de Vasconcelos, he was truly a Christian Spiritist. (Publisher's note).

work *Sacris Solemniis* and set to music by César Franck in 1872, creating a psychosphere of extremely high vibrations.

Dr. Guimarães was led to the center table. Next, to everyone's delight and amazement, the Poverello of Assisi[8] himself entered, accompanied by Sister Clare[9] in the splendor of her youth and beauty, and a few other companions of his revolution of love in the past...

The saint radiated transcendent goodness, such as we had never experienced before. His face was soft and kindly; he was clad in the worn robes of his early days of ministry on the earth, and the air vibrated with tender, harmonious and colorful energies.

Greeted at the entrance by a previously organized committee, the two apostles – spouses of *Sister Poverty* – were led to the table.

We were ecstatic, breathing at an unusual rhythm.

After the opening prayer by our governor, Lopes Netto introduced our director, Dr. Guimarães, speaking briefly about his responsibilities and a few of his biographical traits.

The esteemed scientist, depicting his noble character, approached the podium and began his message:

Noble mentors that honor us with your presence.
Dear brothers and sisters in Jesus-Christ:
Let us praise the Lord and sing hosannas to Him!
The law of progress is incontestable, and the love of our Father is immeasurable, giving everything and everyone continued spiritual growth, which will take them to the heights of fullness.

---

[8] St. Francis of Assisi – I.R.
[9] St. Clare of Assisi. – I.R.

As noted by Jesus in the prophetic sermon *recorded in chapter 13 of the Gospel of Mark, we are living in the time of signs representing major changes that will take place on the earth for ages to come.*

Subsequently confirmed by John the Evangelist in his memorable Book of Revelation, *we are already living in those significant days, heralds of the great transformations that have been taking place on the beloved orb.*

Long before them, Isaiah, Enoch and other prophets also pointed out the events that must happen, thanks to which a new world rich with blessings would come to humankind.

Moreover, the Mayan calendar also accurately marks severe suffering for earth's inhabitants in this period.

Nostradamus, the most famous of prophets, had occasion to foretell the pain-filled events that would befall human beings if they continued their willful behavior.

More recently, Edgar Cayce predicted striking changes in earth's geography in various parts of his own country and others as a result of seismic phenomena decisive for the new world...

And throughout history, revelations concerning the dire events that have been taking place everywhere have increased, grabbing the attention of human beings, who, nonetheless, remain careless, absorbed by the fumes of pleasure and exhausting gratifications.

The Spirits of the Lord also informed Allan Kardec of this matter as he was codifying their teachings, explaining that tragic events would assail the planet, shaping its physical, moral and spiritual structures.

Periodically, worthy prophets and sensitives have expressed their sentiments and concerns about the major changes already taking place, but which will become even more significant should society continue on its unbridled rush into moral disasters caused by their unyielding self-centeredness.

Such fatalism is expressed as the effect of our continued primitive behavior, far from the liberating teachings presented by Jesus, easily applicable to the moral and spiritual concepts prevailing in a society gripped by ignorance and materialism, even that which is theoretically linked to certain religious beliefs.

In a way, the landscape of the revelations is Dantesque, wanton.

In spite of the extremely valuable information concerning the tragic events, there is much ignorance about what will happen afterwards.

All prophecies, however, state that a better world will arise, a new Jerusalem, lands flowing with milk and honey, a paradise of light and beauty: the very kingdom of heaven on earth itself...

...And that revelation has been forgotten because the human spirit is still purposefully or not dominated by what is terrifying and threatening, oblivious to the largesse of love and mercy of God towards His creatures.

When John the Evangelist heard the serious revelations, his heart was heavy and he asked: "Is there is no hope?"

The beloved disciple was greatly distressed, but he soon heard the beautiful answer: "There is always hope, O thou, for whom heaven and earth were created."

A second possibility is part of the divine plan as long as humans meet the expectation of love, generating new resources regarding the Good, which will produce uplifting effects.

Thus continues the great seer of Revelation: "But I did not see what happened to them, because my vision changed, and I saw a new heaven and a new earth, for the first heaven and the first earth had passed away." Emotion took the apostle, who rejoiced when he heard a great voice (of angelic beings) saying: "There will be no more death, neither sorrow, nor crying, and neither shall there be any more pain."

There was an encouraging pause, reducing the concerns of the audience regarding the afflicting events ahead.

Personally I had always dwelled on the revelation of despair and not on the resultant effects when the time of bliss would arrive on the renewed world after the great calamities.

Then, the esteemed messenger continued:

These blessings will occur because spirits uncompromised by evil will be on the planet building the kingdom of heaven in hearts and working effectively for solidarity based on love.

They will speed up moral progress, using intellectual and technological means to promote fraternity among peoples so that the more powerful will help develop the less endowed, replacing war with solidarity, and the perverse, clandestine slave trade with freedom of choice and exchange, and fighting pandemic, endemic and degenerative diseases, which will have no place, because members of the noble family will not be marked by large debts...

Once the planet's constitution is renewed, its tectonic plates harmonized, the high temperature of its volcanic magma decreased, the many cataclysms that have assailed and destroyed it will gradually disappear. The temperature will become stable, without searing heat or freezing cold, and its landscapes will be Edenic.

Once the physical body adapts to the new climate conditions, it will undergo special changes, also due to the beings that will inhabit it, imprinting other physio-psychological values that will contribute to its spiritual evolution.

It will be in these bodies that multitudes of beneficent visitors will reincarnate to contribute to the progress of humanity.

Concomitantly, due to their thoughts and inner enlightenment, those able to enjoy the time after the great transition will no longer have needless organs, and will have graceful, light forms compatible with the future physical and moral atmosphere of a happy earth.

At that time, hardened warriors and troublemakers, brothers and sisters who cause disorder and conflict, those who take pleasure in championing evil will be transferred to another planet in tune with their vibrations, a planet whose psychosphere is compatible with their condition, receiving them into temporary exile, where they will use their technological know-how to assist its native inhabitants. They will suffer the pain of longing and separation from loved ones, and will prepare themselves morally to ascend and return to the earth...

One's values are never lost before the Divine Codes. The Most-Loving Father watches over the universe, having delegated to Jesus the creation and governance of the earth, which He has been guiding with ineffable love and unparalleled compassion so that we, its inhabitants, may rid ourselves of the imperfections that hold us back and, as prodigal children, may return to His flock.

Emotion-filled silence again permeated the room. Diaphanous light adorned him as he spoke in a gentle, unforgettable voice:

Many of us have been equipping ourselves with knowledge in the fields of genetics, embryology and embryogenesis in order to prepare the bodies that will host, in the cloister of motherhood, those messengers of love and mercy on their earthly pilgrimage.

Our excursion to the beloved planet is meant to prepare society for the sublime endeavor of the great transition.

Time is short, and it is necessary to make up for the days squandered on awful games of illusion.

We need everybody's prayerful help, imploring the holy Poverello to intercede to Jesus for us, His imperfect workers.

Exhorting the sublime mercy of love for all, we appreciate your attention and acquiescence in listening to us, as well as your participation in the future preparatory undertaking of the new era.

May our hearts remain filled with peace.

A profound silence composed of emotion and acknowledgement dominated the entire rapt audience.

Just then, the *Saint of Assisi* stood up, walked to the podium and, enveloped in an aura of sidereal light, prayed, filled with emotion:

Sublime Master Jesus:

Enable us to understand Your will and not our own, surrendering ourselves to Your powerful hands and guidance.

Help us fulfil our responsibilities, but not according to our own desires.

Cast Your gaze upon us so that we have the light of Your tenderness, not the darkness of our ignorance.

Bless our purposes to serve You, even though we have only been concerned about using Your holy name to serve ourselves.

Engage us in the sanctification of Your designs so that You may be in us, for we are not yet capable of being in You.

Subdue our desires for power and pleasure, and help us acquire true renunciation and self-denial.

Help us understand our endeavors, sustaining us in our difficulties and aiding us when we are immersed in the physical body.

Bestow upon us the gift of Your peace so that we may distribute it wherever we may be, that all may behold it and know that we are Your dedicated servants...

...And since death has restored us to the glorious life so that we may continue on the path of enlightenment, favor us with wisdom for the successful journey of ascension, even if we often have to be immersed in the darkness of matter, though led by the compass of Your affable heart pointing the way.

O Lord!

Intercede to the All-Loving Father for us, Your backward brothers and sisters, defectors from duty.

Those last words were uttered with a voice choked by emotion.

At a signal from Lopes Netto, the organist began playing.

Flakes of light descended gently to the rhythm of the melody, and we automatically began embracing each other, following the example of the noble members at the presiding table.

The meeting ended with a special wave of tenderness and beauty.

14
Guidelines for the Future

We were all ecstatic after the mentor's speech and the *Saint of Assisi's* prayer. It seemed we all feared that the vibration of transcendent love that filled the auditorium and flooded us inside might be broken.

When we finished embracing one another, we approached the head table in single file because everyone wanted to meet, even if briefly, the venerable benefactors attending the meeting.

Approaching slowly and orderly, when our turn came Lopes Netto told Dr. Guimarães that Ivon and I would be accompanying him on the excursion to the physical world.

He smiled cheerfully and embraced us with the benevolence of a loving father who seemed to know us from before, perhaps...

I could not utter one single word to him, yet I was able to hear him in the recesses of my mind and heart.

I soon came to know that he would remain on our plane, from where he would be directing the endeavors of the groups, each one having a leader that would represent him.

Then we approached the Saint of Assisi, and I could not resist his tenderness. I was overcome with spontaneous tears, demonstrating my smallness before his greatness.

Uncommon humility and a smile of affection and compassion floated in his eyes and face, facilitating our exchange of love.

I kissed his charity-sanctified hands and could only manage to say, trembling, "God bless you! Thank you very much!"

I was saturated by his tenderness for a long, long time afterwards.

Before the two messengers from Umbria returned to their dwellings of light, Lopes Netto said that, in about 15 minutes, all the groups, according to his previous instructions, should meet at their designated spot in that same building in order to receive instructions from their respective leaders.

Hustle and bustle ensued, but devoid of turmoil and disorganization, with each team heading for its indicated sector.

Ours was composed of twenty spirits dedicated to the work of disobsession and spiritual instruction, some of whom were also from the Department of Reincarnation. They had participated in making preparations for the undertaking, having been trained in the mechanisms of fertilization and conception.

When we arrived at the room where we would receive the relevant guidelines, we got to know the different members more intimately.

All were excited and eager to serve the cause of the Good with extreme devotion, feeling blessed for taking part in the construction of the new world.

Unarticulated melodies hung in the air, like onomatopoeia of the night coruscating with stars.

Dr. Guimarães was assisted by the various instructors that would represent him on each team, while he himself would oversee all the labors from our community.

Thus Dr. Silvio Santana introduced himself to us. Dr. Santana was a devoted staff member from the Department of Reincarnation. In his last incarnation, he had been a dedicated obstetrician and geneticist, a scholar of human reproduction.

It was his duty to enlighten us regarding a few aspects of the endeavor to which we would dedicate ourselves for the next eight weeks. When he finished, he answered a few of our questions.

We would be participating in selecting couples to receive visitors from other realms as their children so that they could achieve their superior goals, starting the cycle of rebirths on the earth until the time the beacons for the era of regeneration were established.

We would be utilizing couples who longed for parenthood but who, due to various reasons, were having difficulties conceiving, thus resorting to artificial conception with subsequent implantation of the egg, making possible the reincarnation of spirits who would work for the Good on the earth undergoing renewal.

Moreover, we would be giving moral and spiritual assistance to the prospective parents so they would not allow themselves negative influences or connections to the perverse spirits swarming on the planet's surface, some idle, some vengeful or jealous, and a much larger percentage disruptive for the sheer pleasure of it.

I could just imagine the huge significance of the spiritual exchange between the two spheres of life, and I understood the power of love in the building of society, love which is always the same whether one is in the physical body or outside of it.

The meeting proceeded in a loving atmosphere with prospects for much activity.

About two hours later, we were scheduled to meet in the Ecumenical Temple plaza, whence we would all descend to the different cities of our beloved Brazil.

Each team would be responsible for operating in a specially selected area, while all would remain connected with Dr. Guimarães, who would have his headquarters in the region geographically close to the capital of Minas Gerais.

When we arrived at the plaza to start our journey under the blessings of the twinkling stars, we were invited to say a prayer formulated silently at the heart of our best sentiments.

Then we boarded the vehicles that would take us to the previously prepared centers that would serve as headquarters for our activities, repose, planning, evaluation and studies.

Actually, other caravans had already been visiting the earth for the same purpose since the 1970s and 80s, preparing for the invaluable incarnations to come. However, now was the time to intensify the exchange between earth's inhabitants and the visitors from Alcyone,[10] who were already active in the planet's psychosphere waiting for the appropriate time.

I was informed that a large number of them were in colonies close to the earth, adjusting to the planet's psychosphere and its inhabitants, visiting Spiritist societies

---

[10] Alcyone is the brightest star in the Pleiades Cluster. It is approximately 440 light years from Earth. http://space.about.com – I.R.

connected to the higher spheres, and explaining their reason for being there.

Thus we felt great elation being involved in a well-managed, rigorous program of action focused on the future of society.

Ivon and I were closer to each other, in spite of the spontaneous friendship that connected us with the rest of the team.

Our first activity was scheduled for the following evening, when more than ten thousand discarnate aliens would gather on a Brazilian beach to hear Dr. Guimarães give a speech regarding the commitments of self-enlightenment and spiritual development of the earth.

Thus we spent our time informally, visiting still-incarnate family members, Spiritist institutions dedicated to the ministry of disobsession, and Spiritist psychiatric hospitals, in order to observe the application of invaluable resources of the doctrine on behalf of their patients.

Whenever we are engrossed in our work, time is short and never seems sufficient to do everything that has to be done.

We enjoyed the pleasure of socializing with other spirit friends involved in such endeavors, renewing ourselves inwardly and rejoicing in their blessed achievements until we realized it was time for us to attend to higher duties.

We happily headed for the Brazilian coast, a stretch located between the sea and the mountains, rich in plankton and pure vibrations, uncontaminated by minds in disarray, nor an atmosphere overloaded with poisonous gases.

The clear night enriched by the sounds of nature was an invitation to reflection and prayer.

Thousands of spirits were waiting on the vast stretch of sand tenderly washed by the waves.

It was a natural amphitheater, like Jesus had used many times, from the time He gave the Beatitudes to the sublime encounter on Mt. Tabor, or when He spoke on the shores of the Sea of Galilee, assisting the crowds starving for bread, peace and light...

We could hear the music of the evening breeze and feel the vibrations of harmony that hovered in the air.

Dr. Guimarães stood atop a volcanic stone on the beach, accompanied by various team leaders and a number of assistants unknown to me.

After a prayer anointed with love and faith, our mentor began:

"The great and noble days of the Lord of the Vineyard have arrived.

"You have come from another dimension to work with the Liberator of consciences and you have accepted the task of helping build the era of peace and love.

"You are accustomed to the harmony of your own world, where there is no more suffering, despair, crime or heinousness.

"You will face difficult battles as you deal with violence and rebelliousness, remnants of the primitivism that still prevails in countless individuals on our planet.

"You will be asked to demonstrate fraternity when conflicts and disagreements erupt. You will face outright animosity amongst those with whom you will live. You will have to bear the painful weight of the constant dissatisfaction of those that will be part of your family and activities. You will use the instruments of friendship to struggle against stubborn and fierce hatred. You will have to understand your assailants, who never seek to understand the other and who always think they are right. You will suffer slander and defamation, unhealthy competition, and the ingratitude of those in whom you deposit your trust and benevolence. They will twist your words and will threaten you in the most cowardly ways. You will experience disgrace and humiliation... Even so, Jesus will be with you at all times.

"You will walk on rock-strewn pathways marked by impediments, but that will not be a problem for you because you are used to overcoming obstacles and ascending the heights.

"In all situations, remember that you are guests on a planet in transition, invited to make it a paradise after the continuous storms that will shake it.

"You will triumph if you remain faithful to love and fraternity, open to compassion and mercy.

"Go visit the homes where you will dwell, practicing patience and courage alongside your future families unaccustomed to the standards of goodness and justice, understanding and equality.

"Let yourselves be emotionally touched by the agonizing brothers and sisters that still swarm on our beloved planet. Comfort them, and inspire them with the joy of living and with gratitude to God for the opportunity for moral and spiritual growth.

"You will be *the salt of the earth*, maintaining its taste in order to make the days you live in the somatic body better.

"You will experience the limitations of the physical body, trying to trap you in the heavy robes of matter; however, during your hours of physical rest, you will return to our sphere of action, where you will be comforted and encouraged to continue your missionary endeavor.

"Ambassadors of the Good, remain in the battle for Peace, always loving, and never armed with any emotional weapon of belligerence or animosity.

"Welcome to the earth!

"May God bless your ministry planned by Jesus!"

There was a silence composed of joy and hope.

Other supervisors made brief comments concerning the phenomenon of rebirth, using material written by the beloved geneticist, referring to some problems with fertilization and conception when the egg stays attached to the wall of the uterus.

References were made to the great achievements of modern sciences that study human reproduction, and suggestions were made that prayer, as the science of exchange with the Divine, be used as much as possible.

After introducing the program to all the future reincarnates and us, the workers involved in the preparation, we mingled with guests and other teams, addressing considerations about the unusual endeavor designed for the future.

An unrestrained joy visited all of us, maintaining the expectation of a successful enterprise.

The time came for us to return to our fields of activity and rest, while the visitors, lovely in appearance and bearers of wisdom, headed for their destinations.

We bid farewell to Dr. Guimarães, with whom we would not have many more opportunities to interact due to his grave commitments.

I was able to observe a number of incarnate spirits partially disengaged from their physical bodies through sleep moving about in our world of vibrations without the slightest inkling of it, incapable of any lucid contact and immersed in their usual interests, holding on to the same passions and sentiments as when awake in the physical body.

At other times, however, I could see the lights of truly high order spirits that visited the earth, coming or returning, like divine lights blessing the vast dark night invading the planet in that area.

15
Enlightening Experiences

Before returning, we superficially got to know the spirits who would be under our mentor's guidance, and whom we would assist with their rebirth in dense matter.

According to Dr. Santana, there were about a thousand of them. They would also accompany us to the encampment built by experts that had preceded us.

The plan indicated a meeting between the visitors and the incarnates at the first opportunity, and one was set for the following night.

Throughout the day we conversed with some of them and listened to their wonderful stories about the life they enjoyed on Alcyone.

The words in my vocabulary are insufficient for repeating their narrations, transmitted through mental projection, giving us an imperfect idea of the splendor of the kingdom that awaits all of us on the sublime march of evolution.

I could grasp what Jesus meant in John 14:1-2 when he said, "Let not your heart be troubled; believe in God, believe also in me. In my Father's house are many mansions."

It could be no other way. If the earth were the only world privileged with people, the billions of stars spinning in the universe, producing an unending, majestic symphony of creation, would be useless...

Invariably, we have dwelled on information about conduct disorders and obsessions, sufferings of all kinds, incompleteness, regions of trial and purgation, areas of expiation and untold torment after the grave. The reason we have done so is in order to awaken the sleeping consciousness of incarnate spirits committed to wrongdoing instead of inner rehabilitation; sailing against the current, instead of heading for the safe port... However, regarding physical and spiritual constitutions of happy worlds, we lack the words to translate their beauty and harmony.

In our sphere of spiritual action, for example, the landscapes are rich with incomparable tonalities, sunrises and sunsets imbued with lights of indefinable hues, gardens, springs gushing crystal-clear water, flowers in multicolored garlands and sweet, penetrating fragrances, schools and theaters for intellectual and moral training, exemplary hospitals and sanatoriums that will inspire future buildings on the earth – as is already happening – and art galleries in all genres, where fine artists hone their skills in order to render the earth a paradisiacal planet...

Laboratories for planning and projects for discovering the Laws that govern the planet and the cosmos, diligent work to eradicate the diseases and disorders that still predominate on the planet, and meetings enriched with wisdom entailing lofty discussions and conversations about life and its existential purpose...

Universities for delving into the most advanced knowledge, preparing teams of spirits illuminated by love and cultural information with the mission of preparing new and successive generations for the future of a happy humanity...

Spectacles of light and sound in direct contact with nature, which itself is dressed in precious, vibratory garb to edify and help us bless her with our gratitude; high-quality plays and poetry, not to mention living libraries filled with books that bear the images of those who wrote them, including their emotions; video libraries and virtual images on special computers, and superior television broadcasts communications – all meant for the ennoblement of individuals and their inner achievements...

There are also rooms, not always available to everybody, where the past experiences of the local inhabitants are archived. The only ones that have access to them are those who have attained a significant level of evolution so that, consulting the past, they can plan the future, overcoming their innermost conflicts...

Life is a hymn of immeasurable magnitude honoring the Creator.

Even when it imposes rehabilitation through suffering, the beauty of justice is rewardingly expressed, offering hope and opportunity to all, an incontrovertible demonstration that only love exists everywhere, presenting itself, according to each individual's and society's level of evolution, as the essence of life, fundamental for preserving the immortal spirit.

In their narrations, the new alien friends spoke of emotions that we have not yet experienced. They described iridescent landscapes completely unknown to us, sounds and harmonies we have never experienced, their constructions made of modulated energy, whose composition I could not grasp, as it was easily manipulated by the spiritual mind.

The fraternity they described was sublime in a way I had never imagined possible.

The interdependent harmony between the flora and fauna highlights the glorified spirit devoid of organs that break down – although still in the temporary physical garb, but with a view to the infinite progress reserved to it.

In one of their mental projections, we could see a dazzling sanctuary of prayer dedicated to exalting and giving thanks to God, and where the guides of the first-magnitude star communicate with one another, glorifying the Creator.

In addition, what also grabbed my attention was the continuous activity, the ceaseless work of spiritual growth, because uselessness, idleness and enjoyment without making a contribution are deceptive constructions from sickly thoughts and emotions.

In talking with some of the more accessible ones, we were told that reincarnation would somehow entail a grand effort of love on behalf of terrestrial humanity, since they would feel *smothered in the dense body*, limiting them in every way. However they had very willingly offered to contribute to earth's spiritual development without considering it to be a terrible sacrifice.

To leave their realm of splendor for one of darkness, even if for a brief period, was a living demonstration of the power of love, just as Jesus had done, inviting us to do the same.

The large amount of information they transmitted to us during the time before our first endeavor together indelibly impregnated my inner being, providing me with the dream of someday reaching one of those dwellings myself, naturally accompanied by loved ones from the long evolutionary journey, for there can be no paradise, wherever we may be, without the presence of those who have always shared in our struggles and sufferings...

The future, therefore, belongs to us and calls us to advance.

The night had become full and sleep had come over most of the terrestrial inhabitants of the area where we would be operating.

Distinguished spirits from our plane were in charge of bringing approximately 250 couples, partially disengaged from their physical bodies through sleep, to our encampment.

They were lovingly brought in natural torpor to the huge pavilion reserved for them, where they awakened gently, maintaining the relative lucidity of their particular evolutionary state.

Always accompanied by one of those in charge of bringing them to our sphere and caring for them while there, they became aware of what was happening to them. Later, they would recall such occurrence as an unusual dream, whose content would remain imprinted in the core of their being.

In less than half an hour we were all in the room, forming a large audience listening to explanations by Dr. Santana.

The future reincarnates were first made comfortable in one wing of the huge auditorium; we assistants were seated on the opposite side, and the recent arrivals from the physical realm were seated in the middle.

The eminent geneticist began after a cordial greeting:

"We are all gathered here for the first spiritual contact in order to define guidelines for the future.

"All of you who have been brought here nourish the desire to procreate, some of whom have already experienced it.

"A new era has begun for earthly society and, due to your personal merit, you have been invited to participate in that grand event.

"Your lives have been wholesome; your conduct is based on the ethical values of the Good; you are committed to your various religious denominations, and you are striving to find peace and wholeness...

"It is natural, therefore, for you to be chosen to receive some of the missionaries of the future as your beloved children.

"We are living at a very critical time for earthly society, one marked by violence, moral waywardness, drug addiction, vice, and perverse and destructive social norms, all in disrespect for the Divine Codes, nature and its creatures.

"Understandably, by imposition from irrevocable force of the law of progress, a new world of harmony has been planned, a world which will be implemented slowly as the dense darkness of ignorance and cruelty predominating everywhere becomes diluted.

"You will be part of that renewal at a time when pain-filled events will afflict countless families and end many lives, when sentiments of solidarity and compassion will be lacking due to the pursuit of pleasure and the escape from reality.

"Nonetheless, you will be educating those who are going to modify that gloomy landscape and open up brightly lit areas in the dense darkness.

"The children entrusted to you temporarily will need emotional and spiritual support for the desideratum for which they will be sent to the earth.

"Have courage and meet the sometimes bitter circumstances with zeal for the Good and the Truth, protecting them from the initial assaults of their pathway, like watchful farmers defending their seedlings from destructive pests.

"Teach them devotion to duty, responsibility, love and knowledge so that they have the means to fight until victory is achieved.

"The Lord, who has called you, has been taking care of you, for you were reborn at this moment, having been selected for the fulfillment of venerable prophecies regarding the happy era for the humanity of the future.

"Preserve your balanced behavior, your respect for your partner so that you may provide genetic resources suitable for shaping the future bodies of these wayfarers of the light.

"Don't ever be afraid; love as sowers in charge of a duty, without thinking about immediate results. The harvest belongs to the future.

"Keep Jesus in mind and heart, preserving the sentiments of honor learned in your schools of religious faith, convinced, however, of your immortality.

"You will be introduced to those who will soon be asleep in your arms, fully delivered into your care for the tasks they are to fulfill.

"May the Lord Jesus bless us all!"

Immediately we saw a large screen, on which were written the couples' names. Beside the names was a kind of virtual photo with the name of the one who would be their child.

A member of our team then began to call out their names, inviting them to approach the wide, empty area between the audience and the platform containing the head table.

When the name of the couple and spirit – their future descendant – was called out, the escorts who had brought the incarnates went over to the spirits and led them into the large area, where the couples and spirits embraced and talked joyously.

Everything was done in an orderly way without any commotion, despite the large number of individuals being called in a relatively short time to meet one another.

The loving get-acquainted session would last for about fifteen minutes, after which they would embrace each other before returning to their seats.

Our visitors from Alcyone had been informed beforehand about the time required for the first contact and did not exceed it.

After returning to their seats, emotionally renewed and jubilant about the expectations for the future, we heard the *Libera me* from the final part of Franz Von Suppé's wonderful *Requiem*.

The mentor returned to the podium, and demonstrating on his face the gravity of his responsibilities, he took advantage of the lofty atmosphere of peace and hope:

"My beloved brothers and sisters:

"Vested with the noble mission you incarnates and discarnates will perform on the earth, maintain your serenity and trust in God.

"You are responsible for renewing the blessed terrestrial planet as it exits the darkness and enters the divine light.

"You have come from a first-magnitude star, where exalted concessions of love reach a point of unmatched happiness, and you will become immersed in carnal fog, experiencing the difficulties inherent to the limiting human condition.

"You will be temporarily incarcerated in the corporeal diving-suit that, for a while, will curtail your beautiful flights over the sublime landscapes to which you are accustomed.

"You will experience longing for the loved ones you left behind on your merciful journey, oftentimes in apparent loneliness.

"Let me repeat that you will experience misunderstandings and you will suffer the daggers of inferiority that prevail among terrestrial travelers in their momentary moral backwardness.

"At other times, in the partial disengagement of the spirit from its physical body through sleep, you will enjoy time with us. We will be at your side and will take you, although briefly, to those sanctified places whence you have come in order to renew your strength and find the joy to continue your redemptive ministry.

"You will recall the sublime lessons you learned on your blessed home, applying your knowledge in building the imperishable Good amongst your terrestrial brothers and sisters.

"Asphyxiated at times by the sickly fug of the psychosphere of the planet in transition, you will long for celestial vibrations, which you will enjoy again only when your unusual labor of love and sacrifice is concluded.

"You will be characterized in the world by your moral qualities, your psychological content of peace and reflection from the very first days of your new experience.

"Missionaries who have preceded you on the journey to the earth are widening the studies on the psyche and emotions in order to offer you the skilled resources for externalizing your heritage of wisdom.

"New perspectives will be opened to your ministry in the gifts of a loving home rich in tenderness.

"At times people will try to crucify you on the crossbeams of wickedness, but you will triumph out of love."

Discreet tears streamed from the eminent guide's eyes.

After a brief pause, he continued:

"You others, who will receive our visitors as children, and are committed to grow with them toward God: be prepared.

"You know that human reproduction is under severe impositions with respect to the organic constitution, and that the evolutionary needs of each being are designed in the DNA. Nonetheless, it is always the spirit itself who selects the sperm most compatible with its evolutionary purposes.

"Due to the vibration it emits, the spirit selects it from all the others and fires it toward the egg for the miracle of fertilization.

"Heredity is in some ways linked to the physical constitution in a few morphological and biological characteristics. However, the moral strata are provided by the reincarnating spirit.

"Maintain affection and respect in your closest relationships so that you may avoid the meddling of vulgar and pernicious spirits, who will try to hypnotize you to make you adopt vices and aberrations in vogue in marital relations.

"We need your healthy contribution to succeed in the endeavors from the very start.

"Before the rebirths of our spirit guests begin, you will maintain psychic contact with them so that you can develop the sentiments of affection.

"More often, they will be visiting you, adapting to the planetary consciousness and to your emotions.

"Rejoice, workers of the new world!

"You will be living in the great twilight of the current civilization, but you will enjoy the beauty of the dawn of a new era of peace and blessings.

"Cultivate the noble sentiments of duty, harmony and the Good in the various segments of society, and let yourselves be caressed by the spiritual breezes that will carry away the heavy vibrations of the transition period.

"Blessed with this opportunity, begin to plan and think about love."

He made a very brief pause, and then ended:

"Many of you have longed unsuccessfully for parenthood...

"Due to reasons that have come from former times, you have not been able to conceive, but provided for by the messengers of the Lord, the invaluable achievements of genetic engineering will help you achieve the sacred desideratum.

"Lift up your hearts and go back to your human obligations, haloed with happiness and hope.

"The Lord be with you!"

Sidereal harmonies pulsated in the auditorium and in our hearts.

The guides of the reincarnated participants led them back to their bodies, leaving them with lingering memories of the unusual event.

16
Reincarnation Programming

The beginning of the New Era programmed by Jesus for the beloved planet also foresaw the return of philosophers and sages from the past, some of the ancient prophets, various creators of religions, pre-Socratics, and high-order Spirits from the 4th century B.C., such as those that preceded the birth of the Messiah, reincarnating in ancient Rome to make preparations for His advent... Likewise, the enlightened thinkers of the Neoplatonist School of Alexandria, culminating in the 3rd and 4th centuries with the martyrs, with the self-deniers, the medieval saints, the glorious warriors of the Renaissance, the Reformation, the Counter-Reformation, as well as the daring builders of the 17th, 18th and 19th centuries...

Among them, the great missionaries of Science and Technology, rendering the present century a veritable sanctuary of love, beauty, charity and spiritual enlightenment...

Indeed, at different times missionaries of the Good and the Truth have lived on the earth so that there would never be a lack of higher teachings to provide liberation from the shackles of the perturbing tendencies arising from *bad inclinations*. Presently, however, something special is happening in relation to the foolhardy and wicked; those who still delight in wrongdoing; those who, despite enjoying the blessed opportunity of self-redemption, are not taking advantage of it due to their attunement to primitivism. These will be transferred to lower worlds compatible with them.

On those new battlefields, they will bring the knowledge they amassed on the earth, and they will endure the consequences of their stubborn persistence in crime and heinousness until they fulfill their commitments to spiritual growth and are able to return to Mother Earth to take part in its program of sublimation.

A true spiritual revolution has been going on in the world of causes – the spirit world – so that the advent of love and charity, goodness and mercy may take place gradually, in accordance with a very well prepared schedule that can no longer be postponed.

In fact, luminaries of intelligence and love have never stopped reincarnating on the terrestrial world periodically to continue their labors, their increasingly refined specialties, bringing progress and happiness to human beings in the process of ascending toward God.

Connected by love to the work of the planet's intellectual and moral development, they have been shining stars on dark nights, decreasing the darkness and bringing light to the celestial canopy...

They are the ones who do not let us forget our commitments to the truth. They are examples of selflessness and devotion that enrich us with knowledge and loving vibrations so that we may not grow faint in our personal struggles... Some anonymous, others known, they are characterized by the moral and spiritual conduct that makes them superior to the times in which they lived, designing the future with their examples of sacrifice.

Pondering the days of the future, I could not stifle the desire to contribute in some way to these missionaries of the Good. I vowed to intensify my efforts to serve better, at least during the period of preparing for their rebirths in the physical body.

As I talked with my dear friend Ivon, we expressed our sentiments and pondered the great, unknown battles that would be fought, as, incidentally, has been occurring in the daily lives of all noble lives devoted to duty and truth.

At this point, we were invited by Dr. Santana to visit a number of couples who had agreed to receive brothers and sisters from Alcyone.

On our first visit, in the city of Belo Horizonte, we went to a comfortable residence in one of its upscale neighborhoods, where all was silence. The couple was asleep in the bedroom, partially disengaged from their physical body during physiological sleep, dialoguing with the one who would be their firstborn.

The spouses had been struggling unsuccessfully to conceive.

They had consulted several experts and the answer was always discouraging: there did not seem to be any physiological impediment in either of them; nevertheless their chances were nil.

Upon receiving the suggestion that they try *in vitro* fertilization, they had agreed and were preparing for the commitment using careful, specialized treatment.

They would make their first attempt the very next day, using the sperm of the eager would-be father.

Considering the merit of both spouses, two spirits from the New Era team were appointed to be reborn through the special process.

Thus the couple displayed unrestrained eagerness as they conversed with those that would be reborn through genetic conjunctures.

As Dr. Santana knew what was planned for the couple, he proposed that we initiate the preparatory, auxiliary therapy, inviting us to pray to the Lord of Life for the future parents.

After he offered a moving prayer, bio-energetic resources were applied to the sleeping bodies of both partners in order to facilitate the production of healthy sperm and ova, enabling a successful fertilization.

In spite of the precautions taken at the time, we noticed the presence of some afflicted spirits that had rushed to the couple's residence when they learned about the plans for the visitors' rebirth, as they were, in one way or another, emotionally connected to the couple. In fact, it was an abortion in the past that had created the present difficulty. Although the couple had recovered from the crime, the consequences remained in the wife's perispirit, making it difficult for her to conceive... One of those aborted candidates had been a rejected son, and even though he was no longer resentful, his return was not feasible at the moment due to the current plan.

With much tenderness and kindness, our mentor explained it to him and reassured him about his own future, when he too would reincarnate, enjoying better resources for personal progress.

When our task with that couple was over, and as we were headed for another home in one of the outlying districts of the same town, I asked the doctor about *in vitro* fertilization or *test-tube babies.*

He patiently explained to all of us that the always-merciful Divinity incessantly sends His ambassadors to the earth to facilitate scientific and technological progress in order to provide humankind with skilled resources capable of helping them reduce their afflictions.

"Science and Technology join hands all the time," he informed us, "contributing to a happier society. Moreover, missionaries of love are sent so that the sentiments of kindness, mercy and fraternity may reign where there used to be wars of extermination. Of course the horizontal victory of cultural and technical values is easier than the greater, vertical victory of love toward God, which is why there are still heinous wars of every kind.

"Thanks to the birth of Louise Brown, the grand experiment of fertilization outside the human body was successful in 1978. It was a highly meaningful step for individuals unable to achieve conventional fertilization, enabling the transfer of embryos to women suffering from infertile or obstructed tubes. With time and the perfecting of the techniques, it was possible to address other problems that hindered the glorious achievement of motherhood.

"*In vitro* fertilization requires special precautions, starting with therapeutic procedures that induce ovulation so that several eggs ripen, which will allow follicular growth. In special cases, specific drugs are used, which did not occur in the case in question.

"After this painstaking process, the eggs and semen are collected almost simultaneously, more or less in the same period, and after the analysis and selection of the former, insemination with the chosen sperm takes place.

"Special attention is maintained for three days afterward for the transfer of some of the sperm to the uterus.

"This entire process requires perfect identification of maturity of the ova. This is achieved by examining the follicular fluid extracted for this purpose. When the existence of mature eggs in a specialized culture is confirmed, each one of them is inseminated with approximately 100,000 sperm.

"Approximately fifteen to nineteen hours after the procedure, a microscope is used to check for fertilization, which can be confirmed by the presence of male and female pro-nuclei. Twenty-four hours later, the presence of *pre-embryos* can be detected due to division into two cells. Only after forty-eight to seventy-two hours, when there are four, eight or more cells, can transfer be made to the womb.

"In our case, we hope for the success of two out of the many transferred *pre-embryos* to which we will have connected the perispirits of the two reincarnating spirits, who will choose, through special vibration, the sperm that will offer them the specific characteristics for the tasks assigned to them in the physical existence.

"The pre-embryos with no link to future reincarnating spirits will have no purpose and will be automatically eliminated."

The kind geneticist paused for reflection and then continued his amazing explanations:

"Once scholars of the many scientific doctrines seek identification with spiritual revelations, letting themselves understand the mechanisms that build and maintain physical life, it will be much easier for them to fulfill their commitments as missionaries of the Good on behalf of humankind.

"Alongside *in vitro* fertilization, the admirable contribution of women ennobled by love, who lend their wombs for the development of embryos and the emergence of fetuses up to the moment of birth, called *paid surrogate mothers* since they charge for the process, is of indisputable value.

"To help someone achieve motherhood, entailing, on the other hand, the rebirth of spirits, while a large segment of society opts for criminal abortion or uses the so-called *morning-after pill* to stop the process and development of fertilization, these self-sacrificing surrogate mothers play a highly significant role in building the new and better world of tomorrow.

"Although science has achieved this feat for noble purposes, there are always utilitarian and opportunistic persons who use it for financial profit, justifying their purpose as a means to mitigate their financial problems. Although we do not agree with such conduct, we do not oppose them because in some comprehensible cases they are benefactresses of humanity.

"The most curious thing often occurs when, in coexistence with the reincarnating spirit, their dormant sentiments of motherhood awaken, and after giving birth they become emotionally attached to the dear being and refuse to give it up... In some of these cases, we have seen that the reincarnating spirit is more connected to the *surrogate mother* than to the real parents.

"It turns out that no one can circumvent the sublime mechanisms of the cosmic laws that govern the universe and human beings. Usually the transversal paths to which many individuals resort to shirk responsibility lead them exactly to the destiny meant for them and not to the places where they would like to enjoy uselessness...

"Our participation and that of the devoted workers connected with our endeavor will not be permanent. We only take part in special cases, for ever since the latter years of the last century our brothers and sisters from Alcyone have been reincarnating quietly on the earth, becoming exponents of knowledge and making a great cultural and spiritual contribution. As the years have passed since the first occurrences, we are now experiencing the period of *en masse* rebirths, as well as the lengthy purge of unfortunate brothers and sisters connected to rebelliousness and brutality in their futile attempt to prevent human happiness. Likewise, as the years go by, a significant number of obstinate spirits will be sent into temporary exile to contribute to the development of beings on their new homeland, before returning to the earth in triumph after having cleansed themselves of the serious imperfections that had impeded their evolution.

"It has been that way since the dawn of the human races on the earth, when missionaries of love and knowledge from other *mansions in the Father's House* plunged into the planet's darkness to offer their invaluable knowledge.

'*Hence everything is useful; everything in nature is linked together, from the primitive atom to the archangel, who also began as only an atom – an admirable law of harmony, which your limited minds cannot yet grasp in its entirety!*' Thus the high-order spirits responsible for the Codification of Spiritism answered Allan Kardec in number 540 of *The Spirits' Book*. This interconnection had already been perceived by Antoine Lavoisier in his famous quote about the study of mass: "*In nature nothing is created; nothing is lost; everything is transformed.*" Even though it was recently discovered that there is always a loss of mass in the reaction of a substance releasing energy, in no way does that alter the content of our thinking concerning the universal harmony or the Laws that maintain it."

A natural silence ensued, inviting us to deeply ponder the *Divine purposes*.

In the programming regarding the rebirth of the spirits from Alcyone, considering that they have no negative commitments on the earth, the setting of goals for rebirths for paying off moral debts from previous existences was unnecessary, as was always the case in the conventional cases to which we were accustomed.

In the *Department of Reincarnation*, charts drawn up ahead of time portrayed healthy organisms, although subject to the normal decay of energy, as well as occurrences of less serious illnesses, such that for their entire time the spirits could devote themselves to the uplifting labor of fraternity, study, and applications of propositions concerning individual moral and spiritual progress, as well as that of the planet.

Bringing from the dimension whence they came the treasures they had acquired in the process of evolution, they were not exiled for the purpose of rehabilitation, but were volunteers of love contributing to the happiness of the human lives amongst whom they would be reborn.

Therefore in most cases the care with regard to rebirths was limited to the genetic contributions from their future parents so that the candidates' perispirits could mold their intellectual and moral needs, experiencing the environmental conjunctures, but also developing their commitments without major impediments resulting from their organic machinery.

Thus preparations for artificial insemination in the case above continued with the support of Dr. Santana and our team. It became reality days later, when it was possible to transfer the embryos with their respective spirits connected, subsequently giving proof of the pregnancy.

The joy that filled the couple when the two were told of the success became a celebration of love and gratitude to God through prayer, in which we participated that night when they were partially disengaged during sleep.

Both the future parents and the reincarnating twin spirits were ecstatic, dialoguing excitedly and confidently about the plans concerning their spiritual growth through study, dedication to work and unrestricted surrender to the Divine Mercy that provides everything with balance and wisdom.

Based on this and other experiments involving families from different socioeconomic ranks, Dr. Santana stated that it was now feasible to think about *en masse* reincarnations, obeying, however, the determinations of the Lord of Life...

As we worked at our task, we learned about the most dolorous collective discarnations as the result of the planet's convulsions and its geological adaptation. Most of these involved spirits that would no longer be reborn on the earth but, due to the Law of progress, would be transferred compulsorily to a world compatible with their level of evolution.

It was cause for immense elation that we were able to follow the progressions concerning the great transition slowly taking place on the blessed earthly Home, entailing the renewal of millions of spirits who were still ignorant about the Laws of Life, as well as others who were still inextricably entwined in unfortunate moral debts.

We could see the numerous groups of workers from our sphere and others under the high command of Jesus operating on the planet to create a psychosphere compatible with the requirements of the transformations taking place through suffering, as well as through the awakening of consciences by means of knowledge and the blessings of charity.

Spiritist groups devoted to the truth and workers responsible for the general good began receiving specific information about the conduct of their members – which, by the way, has always been the case – in order to create the mental and emotional climate to face the increasing numbers of disasters, accelerating the growth of lives in love and peace.

Meanwhile, recognizing the continuing transformative operations, perverse spirits connected to madness or its victims were fervently at work, developing mechanisms of aggression against all those who were responsible for the ongoing changes.

Expertly organized pitfalls, stereotypes of pleasure, and stimuli of the sensations were inspiring opinion makers and the mass media in order to disrupt the march of progress, increasing excesses of all kinds, especially with respect to servile, easily accessible pleasures.

Insidious, secretive conclaves organized by the enemies of the Good set vengeful goals using corrupt political bodies infiltrated by many of their members, who have reincarnated in that area, as well as in the various religions, the arts and other social sectors, in order for them to wallow in the mire of moral chaos and stimuli against wholesome behaviors, spreading discredit, disrespect for laws and duties, in the lust of accumulating resources that are non-transferrable at discarnation, but deaden the lofty meanings of spiritual existence.

Fomenters of wars of extermination, of insane terrorism, persecution of minorities, of mockery and prejudice have mingled with the multitudes, inspiring calamitous attitudes amongst governments and citizens, such that hope is rudely set aside and lofty examples become messages of profiteers and crazed opportunists...

It was suddenly possible to witness an amazing increase in aberrations, heinous crimes, inclement violence and a lack of authority to stop them or control them, making them banal and almost disregarded.

The "anything goes" principle that has taken root is meant to create a climate of disregard for integrity, ethical values, respect for individuals and society, demonstrating that all these meanings have been lost and that a new, uncontrolled ethic has come to be the standard of behavior for these most unfortunate days...

In fact, a massive wave of pessimism has come to prominence in the ocean of lives, and young people especially, without worthy leadership or guidelines for stability, have become victims selected for their representation as heirs of the future.

Licentious revelry, lewd, vulgar, violent and deceitful TV programs, movies and plays have brainwashed people into thinking that only pleasure at any price is worth it, and have begun to render the earthly stage a place of heinousness, savagery and permissiveness, leading to degradation and exhaustion...

Parents and educators have suddenly become assailed by doubts about the importance of the moral education of children and students as they see the soaring wages with which sickly and shocking behaviors are remunerated in detriment of the decent, tiring professions of those who become exhausted in the course of duty.

The two worlds of vibrations – the physical and spiritual – have increased interaction and have made it easier. Low-order spiritual interchange has become so simple that any mental behavior soon finds a like response in tune with the spirits on that vibratory level. It is clear that the level that relates to the most violent and sensual senses predominates in the general conduct.

Talking with my friend Ivon, we immediately thought of the great battle of Armageddon mentioned in the Bible, which would be symptomatic of the end of the old era, giving way to the new, blissful one, transferred from the valley of the wars of Israel's past to the entire current planet.

Threats of the end of the world, creating fear in fragile minds and emotions, have begun to cause dread, anxiety and despair, just as reasons for using all sensations as a way to forget life and its ills have assumed a prominent role in the various social groups.

Mediums who had committed themselves to the lofty responsibility of using their faculty focused on Jesus are, without realizing it in these difficult times, abandoning the caution recommended by the Master and by Allan Kardec, and have become engrossed in battles of sickly competition, seeking positions of distinction while making themselves instruments of frivolous spirits who delight in prophecies of terror and confused revelations, through which they try to introduce their false information into the Spiritist movement, creating misunderstanding and disorder.

Mutually attacking one another in an exchange of vanity bordering on pride and arrogance, they forget about serving the Spiritist cause, using it for their own conflicting purposes, which they conceal to exalt the tormented and unhappy ego.

Champions of senselessness are invading social groups and are acquiring prestige through well-developed, unscrupulous cunning, acting freely and inciting the insane leaders on their course towards the abyss...

This is all related to the response of the Darkness organized against the programming of the peaceable Lamb, Who does not fight back against evil, but proceeds with methods of love in His desire to promote humankind's progress and their terrestrial cradle.

In our reflections on the following nights, we could see the caravans of luminaries descending towards the earth with the sublime mission of facilitating the reincarnation of the new guides of the future alongside the immigrants from Alcyone in a true symphony of blessings.

On one of these occasions, when, completely silent, our group was out in the open air, I contemplated the glittering canopy of stars and silvery moonlight. Our mentor invited us to prayer, proposing that we totally surrender to the Heavenly Friend who came two thousand years ago to brighten the great night with the luminescence of His ineffable love.

Planetary Transition

As promised, He has been sending, in this moment of so many afflictions, the Comforter, who had already been in the world for over a century as a constellation of high-order spirits so that the darkness could be definitively diluted before the divine sidereal light.

It was impossible to hold back the tears or remain indifferent to the sublime appeals of love.

17
Broadening the Scope of Our Work

Right after Dr. Santana's heartfelt prayer, soft transcendental melodies wafted through the fragrant air of nature, penetrating us deeply and bringing us to tears.

The night had become a backdrop of unusual beauty, and the park, with its trees and flowers, where we were gathered on the beloved planet, received a pilgrim light, which descended upon us, enveloping us and creating a most healthy psychological climate.

Our benefactor stood in this blessed psychosphere, absorbing the gentle vibrations, and enriched by the reigning emotions, began to clarify:

"Dear brothers.

"Jesus has been our sublime Friend and Mentor, our *Guide* and *Model* from the very beginning, leading us to happiness and building the *Kingdom of God* in our hearts. Nonetheless, each one of us is responsible for setting the course to follow. There are those who prefer the flower-strewn paths of the magic of illusion, but those flowers soon demonstrate their fragility by withering when touched by reality. Many others choose disenchantment due to a few natural failures and they descend into the pit of discouragement, surrendering to uselessness and complaining, with which they belittle existence. Still others are enthusiastic at the start but soon give up as they face challenges and difficulties, and lastly, a few stay devoted, working the ground, removing stones, and improving the pathway so as to make it easier to follow by those in the rear.

"The unavoidable law of evolution is inexorable. However, it utilizes the resources of each wayfarer, who chooses what seems best, certain or not of the ultimate results. Having assumed this responsibility, such individuals begin to live according to their chosen directives, subject to the consequences of their decision. These fearless travelers proceed on their journey like an arrow that has been shot and cannot return as it heads toward its mark. Nonetheless, depending on the target, they can redo future shots by changing their trajectory if they have discovered they missed the mark on their first attempt. In view of its options, earthly existence, therefore, has thousands of opportunities to offer its members. All have the right to err, correct it and subsequently reach their goal. Mulling erroneous situations over and over is an unfortunate waste of time that could be used to correct the mistake; moreover, rebelling and complaining increases the load of afflictions, promoting a childish behavior that does not solve anything. On the contrary, it complicates the issue due to the foolishness of the irresponsible acts.

"No one can stop the march of progress, whose object is the fullness reserved for all through God's love.

"Envelopment in the flesh, however, is like a cloud that blurs the sunlight. It produces some forgetfulness of the responsibilities the spirit assumed before immersion in the somatic body, producing conflicts and uncertainties about its reality resulting from misguided behaviors in the past.

"For this and other reasons, some spirits, weakened by a lack of moral strength for facing struggles, let themselves be dragged to the cliffs of darkness, overcome by hatred because of the complicated, unfortunate situations in which they are enmeshed, struggling against the impositions of evolution as if it were possible to impede it, and preventing others from evolving by creating obstacles for them."

There was a gentle quality of enchantment in the benefactor's speech. His face shone with an unknown light, while the ambient harmonies became a framework for his words.

Deeply concentrating on his concepts, we followed his reasoning with special interest.

After a short pause, he continued:

"How many times in our evolutionary history have we enthusiastically assumed commitments to the truth only abandon them soon after, attracted by the smiling myths of pleasure? Believing in our indefinite stay in the physical body, without consciously realizing the presence of infirmities and the reality of discarnation, we wear it out with sensations, poisoning it with disordered emotions and the acid rain of conflicts of a conscience punished by guilt and remorse, which we tried to conceal, complicating the opportunity and making ourselves unhappy. We are reborn many times, with new sentiments of renewal, embracing ideals of recovery; however we soon stumble over the same obstacles, which, due to inertia and imprudence, we dare not remove from our path, thus falling into the same traps promoted by the illusion of pleasure. Faced with the inevitability of new failures, we finally come back incarcerated in blessed expiations imposed on us by Love in Excelsis so that we may appreciate time and opportunity, weakening the strong ties to our previously cherished animality.

"On many such occasions we have found Jesus and we were enthralled with His liberating purpose, His incomparable lessons of love-centered mercy and goodness, surrendering to Him, but not resisting the impulses of our moral inferiority, slowly adapting His teachings to our illegitimate interests.

"In the name of His love, we connected ourselves to imperial power; we stopped being persecuted only to become persecutors ourselves; we abandoned humility under the robes of pride and arrogance... We found ways to alienate the enemies whom we ought to love, the disbelievers we intended to convert, and the confused we should have enlightened, and we began adventures of madness, creating the Crusades, the Courts of the Inquisition, the persecutions of the Moors and Jews, all those who did not share our ideas, sinking into the abyss of the most disastrous aberrations. We culminated such arbitrariness in the name of the Martyr of the Cross with the sale of indulgences, releasing all criminals from their heinous behaviors in exchange for money, which was sent to Rome for building the Basilica of St. Peter and for the Vatican treasures exhausted by the wars of Pope Julius II, who lived more sitting in the saddle of a horse than on the throne falsely called St. Peter's...

"*Indulgences* were an ancient practice that allowed the Pope to mitigate or nullify the sins of the repentant faithful or those who intended to undertake cleansing penance because of their wrongful acts. Nonetheless, Pope Leo X made them official through documents that liberated any sinners from their most heinous crimes by paying the amount set for this purpose. It went as far as to affirm, for example: *As soon as the coin in the coffer rings, a soul from purgatory springs*, in terrible and ambitious disregard for the codes of Christian dignity preconceived and lived by Jesus.

"Amongst these botched experimentations, we tried to impede the advancement of science, vilifying those who opened the horizons of thought to truth, knowledge and freedom, as if we could forever keep an eye on them and set up obstacles in their path, without ever realizing they were being faithful to the commitments we had shirked... It was a psychological mechanism for transferring our frustrations with angry ferocity because they were able to achieve what we did not have the courage to achieve.

"And we made martyrs of thousands of workers of Jesus in the various sectors of thought and ideals, solely because they did not submit to the will of our misguided determinations.

"On the Iberian Peninsula, for example, following the terrible examples in other countries, in the name of Catholic hegemony and fidelity to the pope, we used our ignoble resources to remain in the political, religious and cultural domain of society, expelling from the beautiful lands those we called heretics only because they did not accept our Jesus... Of course they did not accept Him as a result of the examples of anti-Christianity, perversity and presumptuousness with which we represented Him, whereas He let himself be ruled by love, compassion, mercy, forgiveness.

"Long gone on the scale of time are such follies, but their effects still remain in our memory and in our actions. They frequently reappear in manifestations of ferocity when we are contradicted, of repudiation when we are not accepted, of resentment when affection is absent... And we still believe, unfortunately, that this is the best behavior.

"Life, however, representing Cosmic Consciousness, writes the undisputable truth of the Divine Laws on human consciences, and there is no one who can escape its internal presence. That is why we are reaping what we have sown.

"In this critical moment of planetary and human transformations, we are witnessing the great struggle between the forces of the Good and those who say they are members of the forces of Evil, each using the resources that characterize them. While love uses the patience that educates, instruction that enlightens, work that dignifies, and the renunciation of the poisonous passions that debase, hatred – the child of spite and bitterness – sows rage, encourages debauchery, and extends the area of violence in vain attempts to promote aggressive responses... The challengers of iniquity assail without reluctance all those who love duty and progress, seeking to defeat them without any sense of respect for the right to live as they choose.

"Does it not remind us of our devious behaviors in the past? It is therefore understandable that we are targets they want to hit due to the evil we did to them when we had the opportunity to help them get out of the deplorable situations in which they lingered. Their hostile sentiments, still alive *deep within their souls*, result from their resentments since ancient times. Mistakenly, they yearn for retaliation and for peace at the same time, thinking peace will come after they have quenched their thirst for revenge."

Once more he paused briefly and opportunely to give us a chance to follow his information-laden reasoning, before continuing his fascinating thesis:

"We recall historical information asserting that Christopher Columbus received the aid of the Spanish court, when the Catholic monarchs Isabella I of Castile and Ferdinand II of Aragon were happy for having expelled the Moors, who had taken part of Spain in the past. Ever since the seventh century, the country had been carrying out the so-called *Reconquista,* thanks to which Christians and Muslims kept up their perverse and continuous wars. At the end of the 15th century, however, in 1492, the bloody struggles – especially in Cordoba and Granada, the last bastions of invaders – reached the ultimate cruelty perpetrated by the victors. Homes and lives lay in ruins; sanctuaries of faith and religious schools were virtually destroyed and the fury of the insane mob, after towns were burned and survivors hunted down, hoisted the victory flag where the Muslim flag used to wave.

"The Jews were also expelled, their synagogues and homes destroyed, their lives rendered trivial and sold for their weight in gold so that they could remain after apostatizing from their former religion, changing their old names to Christian ones. We entered into agreements with Portugal to transfer many of them to Portuguese lands, where they were imprisoned and mostly murdered by the dominant forces. In that deadly period, the Spanish Inquisition came into being, and the medieval night, which supposedly had vanished, prolonged its darkness for centuries in unimaginable aberrations.

"In order to extract confessions from infidels, every conceivable barbaric means was used, including impalement, the wheel, the rack, and everything heinous that the human mind can conceive when insane. Women were raped; children were killed or sold as slaves, separated forever from their parents; healthy men were also sold; the elderly and sick cruelly killed after excruciating torture... And we would say we did it all in the name of Jesus and His doctrine..."

Suddenly, in the small gap between sentences, we could see tears in his eyes, his voice choked with emotion, increasing our sensitivity.

The onomatopoeia of nature were saturated with joyful fluids that reinvigorated us and bathed the region, renewing the energies of the inhabitants, most of whom were asleep in their homes.

Off in the distance, the moon cast her veil of silver, and the leaves of the trees rustled in the gentle breeze.

The noble mentor continued:

"It is perfectly understandable that the spirits who suffered wickedness at our hands during our rule still harbor a bad memory of our conduct, having plunged into the deep gorges of the lower spirit world, where they started to gather together and build their strongholds, today transformed into almost hellish, though transitory, regions, where they plot the destruction of Christian thought on the earth.

"If we look carefully, we can see how much the Lord's message has degenerated, even today, with sects and denominations multiplying fiercely, each claiming primacy of knowledge and supremacy of the truth, transforming the tithe into what indulgences used to be... Materialistic market resources are used to lure unsuspecting and ambitious customers who want to purchase the Kingdom without their inner transformation for the better, increasing the moral licenses granted to countless so-called modern religious denominations so they can conform to the vulgarity of these days... The Apostolic Roman Catholic Church suffers the madness of the pedophilia of some of its members, priests and prelates, experiencing a highly distressing situation, beyond the temporal power it has enjoyed for more than seventeen centuries...

"... And the disciples of the *Comforter*: how have they been behaving? Are there not already glaring differences in lamentable schisms by currents that adhere to X, Y or Z at the expense of the Kardecian Codification, from which we all draw the liberating knowledge? Do not erring, aggressive, conceited, vindictive, persecuting, and insensate mediums appear daily, claiming supremacy, completely forgetting the lessons of the Excellent Medium of God?[11]

"Moreover, bizarre attempts emerge to update Spiritist thought with disorder instead of joy, with ridiculous displays of reproachable social behavior, with false holistic ideas that mix different concepts in order to appeal to the various religious denominations, with parties and profitable activities abounding in alcohol, with sexually sensual dancing and carnival-like festivities to attract more followers – especially young people – instead of educating and guiding them within the impositions of their temporary youth. Devoted workers faithful to the Codification are mocked and ridiculed in deriding tones as being orthodox, whereas the deriders call themselves modernists, as if spirits were divided either into strict or jesting, austere or playful in the use of the liberating message of the Gospel of Jesus in the light of the Spiritist revelation.

---

[11] Jesus Christ. – I.R.

"Without a doubt, it is the lower human passions that predominate in generating these unfortunate situations... Besides them, however, due to the carelessness of so many individuals who accept these impositions, there is interference by minds opposed to Christ, molding them and inspiring them to demonstrate what they call the "falsehood of the Lamb," thanks to His insane believers. Thus, obsession is rife in many religious arenas, and unfortunately the Spiritist movement is not exempt, because there are a number of reckless and ignorant spirits wanting the projection of the ego as well as positions of importance to free themselves from conflicts by exalting the personality...

"These innovations are worrisome since they foster vices and behavioral license in detriment of healthy and honorable conduct in the service of consoling human suffering and working to eradicate its causes.

"The spectacle, therefore, is programmed in the nefarious regions of the lower spirit world inhabited by those who had been our victims and do not believe in our current values. Moreover, when they test us we fail miserably, adhering to their vulgar and sickly sentiments. Knowing our spiritual weaknesses and sore points – our Achilles' heels – they use our vulnerability to intrude into the ennobling programmings of human conduct, maintaining the clichés of the vices and miraculous solutions of last-minute repentance, of *accepting Jesus* at the end of one's life, wrongfully believing they are going to heaven...

"A revision of current social behaviors is urgent in the religious, political, and artistic communities, in which beauty has been replaced by the erotic, and the heinous crime of abortion has become an act of courage worthy of imitation, proclaimed by opinion multipliers and famous women...

"Like the Stoic times of primitive Christianity, it is urgent to return to the simple, unadorned Jesus, to the pulchritude of His teachings and His natural way of life.

"It is asserted that, because of the advanced technology and the great achievements of science and knowledge in general, there is no room for an innocent, lofty way of life in this day and age, when, in fact, an upright life should be promoted as a natural therapy for keeping people from the pandemic of depression, psychosomatic illnesses, degenerative diseases, violence and aggression, all sorts of crimes, and the interference of low-order spirits in human lives, generating obsessions and various disorders, as regrettable as they are dolorous...

"We, the spirits in the Lord's service, charged with the preparation of the new era, are committed to awakening consciences and to working in consonance with our brothers and sisters in the physical world so that renewal may happen starting now, step by step, reconstructing the moral world far and wide, but especially within, *in the heart whence proceed good and bad words and behaviors* – as the Galilean Rabbi put it.

"This is not a simple task, as indeed nothing is when it comes to lofty values, radical changes from imbalances to order, from error to correctness. Committed to the program outlined by Jesus, let us persevere, giving way neither to frivolousness nor the gilded insinuations proposed by evil.

"*Jesus, today as yesterday, and tomorrow as today* is our motto. Victorious over time, He is waiting for His message to actually be lived as taught by His example. There is no other alternative but to advance on the path of victory over the lower tendencies."

He finished filled with emotion, as we breathed the soothing air of nature's festival of stars…

A profound silence came over us, broken only by the sidereal harmonies…

18
Thoughts and Profound Dialogues

Enthralled by the speech, and aware that the time we had all been anticipating had arrived, Ivon asked the venerable instructor:

"I believe you might be preparing us for experiences that are much more meaningful than our present ones; correct? Your explanations of our responsibilities would lead me to believe that our victims are in need of us in their hopeless environment. Would you mind telling us a bit more?"

We were all eager for the responses to Ivon's timely question.

Without hesitation, Dr. Santana gazed at us with a different glow in his eyes and confirmed:

"Our purpose in presenting such information is to awaken in all the sentiment of responsibility concerning the unfortunate events taking place on the planet and the wave of despair sweeping over it. We see the bloody battles resulting from international terrorism, in which, in the very beginning, East and West confronted each other... We mustn't forget that they are remnants of the tragic Crusades, which led Westerners to loot and pillage at the command of fanatical kings and other semi-barbarians, who, in the name of defending the empty tomb of Jesus Christ, advanced with their armies like starving locusts on the cultural treasures and riches they believed they could take from those they deemed their enemies, without any grounds for such a wrongful conclusion. Rivers of blood ran deep and profound resentment raised barriers between the two cultures, which should have joined each other in order to benefit humanity as a whole...

"More recently, haste – the child of fear and resentment – has triggered one more shameful, hard-to-end war entailing thousands of civilian and military deaths, with escalating complications each and every day.

"From the very first moment, national fanaticism has expanded throughout numerous countries subject to the inclement yoke of other, more powerful ones, encouraging the perverse use of human bombs in inconceivable attacks on themselves and others.

"The spirit armies of the lower realms, which, for the moment, are sowing heinousness on the planet, are led by victims of the disgraceful *Inquisition*, under the command of former Jewish rabbis and Moorish ulemas, who had been thrown into infested dungeons and either tortured to death or burned alive after suffering every kind of torture.

"Still wretched today, ever since the remote days of 1478 in Spain and 1536 in Portugal, when the persecutions began as the result of the papal bull signed by Sixtus IV on November 1, 1478, at the request of the *Catholic kings*, who wanted to restrain – as they did successfully – the so-called Mosaic practices in the form of rites and ceremonies among those called the *new Christians* of Castile and Aragon, in view of the fact that the practices had been spreading due to the tolerance of permissive bishops and other church authorities...

"Through the bulls and inquisitorial edicts, perversity and petty interests spread terror on the Iberian Peninsula and several other countries. Ignorance – that daughter of shamelessness – took to the courts all those that fell into disgrace due to a complaint by someone interested in the victims' spoils, in concordance with prelates and bishops appointed by the kings of Castile and Aragon for such purposes, creating the misfortune that has dragged on until these days of darkness and restoration... The heinous organization would survive until it died out in Spain in 1834 – although it actually still operated until much later – and in Portugal through 1821. And let's not forget the *auto-de-fé* in Barcelona on October 9, 1861, when Spiritist books were burned in the castle esplanade of that Catalan city.

"The love of Jesus has since long ago called us to implement a program to redeem our wrongdoings by seeking those whom we offended, tortured and led into misfortune. Since we are living at a time of spiritual definitions on the earth, we can no longer postpone the opportunity to consciously search and find our brothers and sisters in misery, who remain in the labyrinths of hatred."

"How might we fulfill that programming?" asked Ivon.

The kindly friend elucidated:

"Committed as we are alongside thousands of other groups of spirits working to implement the new era – especially in preparation for the reincarnation of luminaries of the past, as well as our guests from Alcyone – we have been monitoring the hostile siege of the spirits I mentioned earlier, in their efforts to impede the ongoing program.

"Likewise, high-order spirits of philosophy, art, religion and politics of the past – those regarded as the *fathers* of those fields – will reincarnate in order to reformulate, update and lead to the origins of the ideal from which their postulates deviated, facilitating the transition in other segments of society.

"During our current endeavor, we will have the opportunity to be confronted by those deranged spirits who, just as in the old days, when areas were designated for battle, will challenge us to hand-to-hand combat before the applause of idle onlookers, who remained on the sidelines waiting to see who would win in order to join their ranks... Alongside their techniques of indignity and villainy, ours will always be the instruments of love and compassion in the form of charity toward all and ourselves, using the helmet of faith and the flaming sword of goodness so that victory will be that of Jesus uncrucified..."

During the natural silence that followed, Anselmo asked:

"Are we going to continue our present task of helping prepare reincarnations?"

"Yes, of course, because our endeavors may be seen as rehearsals for the mass events that have already been prepared, depending exclusively on the psychic condition of the planet and the responsibilities consciously assumed by the parents who will receive the noble immigrants, as well as the returning missionaries of the past.

"We are on the threshold of the glorious moment announced by the Lord when he was with us, and confirmed by His messengers down through time, who have been waiting for this moment for the final construction of the *Kingdom of God* in all hearts.

"We are the humble, anonymous workers who are preparing the soil for the major inroads of progress so that comfort and happiness may glide in triumph on the beautiful paths that our calloused hands worked when the terrain was difficult and untamed."

Pausing for a moment, the friend and benefactor looked up at the glittering canopy and made note of the light that fell with relative speed toward the planet, illuminating the spectacular night even more.

"They are arriving, greeted by countless workers from the Master's harvest field, placing them in the homes where they will be reborn."

There was a longer pause, leaving nothing else to be added.

Because morning was dawning, Dr. Santana invited us to visit an outlying neighborhood of that same city, where the suffering was more expressed as socioeconomic misery.

We walked among the miserable hovels with open air sewage. Domestic animals were breaking open plastic garbage bags in search of food, attracting voracious rats that would also attack children sleeping on bare, infested boards on the ground.

We went inside one of those gloomy strongholds and I noticed a subtle light coming from a humble construction.

Perceiving my silent question, the benefactor explained:

"That is the residence of Herminio and Rosalinda, a young couple from our sphere. They were reborn into poverty in order to redeem former extravagances, and have pledged to cooperate with the reincarnation from one of the visitors from Alcyone.

"Adherents of Spiritism, they are faithful to the commitments they embraced in the spirit world. They got married a few months ago after their happy reencounter at a nearby Spiritist Center, where they experience comfort and serve selflessly.

"Touched by the teachings of Jesus, they have the wholesome habit of reading *The Gospel according to Spiritism* by Allan Kardec every night before going to bed. It has become a wonderful form of spiritual study and has attracted a significant number of discarnates who work in the area, turning the home into a haven of rest and renewal.

"Let's go inside."

The apartment was very modest and small: a space with a small table with two chairs, a stove, and a sink for cleaning dishes and pans, in addition to a cramped bedroom and a bathroom – all in a space of less than 30 square meters.

The spiritual activity was great, the para-physical dimension much larger than the physical, with a significant number of visitors, among them the members of our group.

Guided by the benefactor, we went into the plain bedroom. The husband and wife were asleep and partially disengaged from their physical bodies, displaying some lucidity and a comforting joy.

Seeming to know Dr. Santana, they embraced him and expressed unexpected joy, externalizing the love of Heaven through its servants on the earth...

Presently, a noble spirit entered, whom I soon identified as an immigrant from Alcyone, displaying an indescribable happiness that was also transmitted to us.

Dr. Santana introduced him to his future, ecstatic parents, who began conversing with him in a special way. While the couple expressed their thoughts verbally, we noticed that the visitor emitted very powerful mental waves that condensed as perfectly understandable symbol-answers.

The visitor said he was strongly interested in enjoying his future, illuminative experience, bringing inner yearnings of love and an immense desire to contribute to the transformation of the planet and its society, that he had prepared himself before coming to Earth in a special vessel in order to observe the level of achievements already attained and to choose the endeavor in which he would be the most useful.

He wanted to be reborn in this stronghold of suffering and need in order to help it ascend to a better condition through his efforts and actions on behalf of the advancement of that suffering community.

We followed the interesting dialogue for several minutes, before he ended with the statement that he would connect with the couple in just a few days, when we would be present to take part in his reincarnation.

He effusively embraced his future parents who were magnetized by his luminosity.

Dr. Santana invited him to accompany us on a visit to another home.

The respectable friend's presence gave a special tone to our group because of his radiations, providing us an uplifting conversation about life in his realm. He used the same method already referred to: while we verbalized our thoughts, he conveyed his through symbolic telepathy.

He described the beauty of the realm in which he had dwelled until recently, the plethora of colors clothing nature, and the indescribable harmony that reigns on that home of indefinable progress. He referred to the absence of suffering as we understand it, the fraternity and coexistence in mutual assistance, the joys and gratitude to the Supreme Creator of the universe, worshiped in spirit and in truth, and the beautiful achievements of intelligence allied with the sentiments.

His externalized thought produced a musical vibration, which we also absorbed, adorning with delicate sounds the images we were able to capture.

In turn, he asked us about the landscapes of gloom and anguish he had noticed on the earth, the dense waves of unhappiness and rebellion that reached him with vibratory jolts, as well as the horror of violence, and the unrestrained pursuit of the dissolute, destructive passions that characterize our *world of trials and expiations* for now.

Without any expression of criticism, he analyzed the primitivism still existing on our planet, where the horrors of war periodically claim millions of lives, the continuous waves of terrorism of every kind, the seismic phenomena that undermine the earth's geological structure, and the superlative suffering...

There was a pained expression on his face as he analyzed the new world where he would be working in an attempt to help it evolve. He became even glummer when referring to crime, the terrible induced abortions, euthanasia, the number of suicides, and the still-legal death penalty.

Lastly, he referred to the tsunamis of a moral nature, which were somehow responsible for the others resulting from the adaptation of the constantly moving tectonic plates.

As Dr. Santana explained things to him and as both commented on the current state of our beloved orb, the more his face displayed tenderness and compassion, expressing the sentiment of solidarity for the world's sufferers, who yearn for deliverance from the tragic attractions and shackles that keep them bound to the primitivism still prevalent in our social and moral culture during these days slowly changing for the better.

Trying to keep the moment from becoming altogether too gloomy and afflictive, the mentor expertly began describing the expectations for the work at hand, as well as the happiness of being able to help construct the Good wherever the vestiges of evil are found.

We immediately felt refreshed, and the sweet enchantment from the presence of our guest animated us again.

Meanwhile, we had arrived at a middle-class apartment in the center of the city. We went in.

One could breathe the psychosphere of peace. There were no vulgar or troublemaking spirits. We were welcomed at the door by the smiling residents, partially disengaged during physiological sleep. They seemed to be expecting us, although I had had no idea we would be going there...

Dr. Santana, always very courteous and ethical, introduced us to the kindly couple, Alonso and Eunice, who were expectant about the possibility of being given the blessing of children.

Initial difficulties inhibiting the husband had been a cause for suffering, but they had been overcome by means of a minor surgery not long ago.

That night, after sexual communion, they were waiting for the divine mercy to enthrall them with the upcoming arrival of a child.

As we conversed joyfully, two workers from another group dedicated to reincarnation entered, bringing the spirit who would wear the physical garb from that moment on.

We all went into the bedroom and stopped before their sleeping bodies, wrapped in the tenderness of an embrace of gratitude and joy...

Dr. Santana approached Eunice, whose heart was illumined by a gentle light while in her body the sperm were moving in her reproductive organs.

The learned geneticist explained to us that it was an amorphous substance in activity, consisting of hundreds of millions of sperm, three million of which could enter the uterus with the ability to survive up to 48 hours. He explained that fertilization takes place within 10 hours, approximately, when the *chosen one* begins its ascent up the vaginal tube through the cervix in order to penetrate the fallopian tube, where it will encounter the egg prepared to receive it.

This *miracle* – he made it clear – is one of the grandest moments of life, which will soon become a human being, something that also occurs with slight differences in the plant and animal kingdoms... When the gametes unite, technically they are endowed with their ancestral inheritances, which we know are established thanks to the *Law of Cause and Effect* through the perispirit.

That said, he approached the woman and applied his hands with the palms facing down, as if annulling the material organization, and called our attention to the inside of her uterus.

Then he asked for the future reincarnate to come closer and think strongly about connecting with the sperm cell that was carrying some of his biological characteristics and some of the father's.

From his *crown chakra* – lit up like a small rainbow around the upper part of the brain – descended a silver ray that penetrated the gelatinous substance and settled upon a tiny gamete, which also absorbed the now bluish light, vitalizing it and making it shoot off from the rest of the group.

Thus began the process that would culminate with the fertilization of the ovum, that is, when it joins the protein receptors in the pellucid, producing an enzymatic reaction that enables the area to be perforated, after which it penetrates the egg and fertilizes it. It is a process that usually takes about twenty minutes, culminating with the displacement of the egg for implantation in the uterus.

Time would take care of the natural process, and from that moment on, our visitor was already psychically linked to the future body that would be shaped by the perispirit.

"The sperm's journey is momentous and full of challenges," explained our mentor, "because the distance to overcome is wide and the trip takes place at about one centimeter per minute, the upper portion of the fallopian tube being located some thirty centimeters away... It also has to withstand the acids that the female organism produces, killing a large number of candidates. Due to the divine purposes of procreation, this acidity decreases during ovulation, which facilitates the survival of many that proceed attracted by the egg."

We observed that, upon connection of the spirit's psyche with the sperm, he experienced a kind of shock, paling slightly and seeming to become dazed briefly; but he soon overcame these emotions and sensations.

He could stay involved with other activities; however the connection with the male gamete would follow its course and fertilization would ensue, followed by the whole process of rebirth in the flesh.

Informed of the event, the prospective parents kissed Dr. Santana's hands and lovingly embraced the one who would be their longed-for son, bringing us all to tears.

The benefactor commented further on the sperm's struggle against the hostile defense mechanism in the female body:

"A modern school of psychiatrists, disciples of the admirable Dr. Melanie Klein, believe that this phenomenon remains in the deep unconscious, causing some behavioral problems that need careful psychotherapy in order to achieve total release from the shock resulting from the battle fought in the period that precedes fertilization...

In the simplicity of the bedchamber, and in light of the cheerful daybreak, the beloved mentor invited us to say a prayer of thanks to God for His ineffable mercy, leading us to a state of near ecstasy, while translating our sentiments at seeing human life in the process of physical development, following the course of its biological destiny.

Participating in such an event, there is no one who will not bend before the divine majesty, the generator of life in its multiple aspects.

Only love has this magical power to command everything and to open the doors to its understanding.

The task finished – one that would be repeated many times in the days that followed – we headed for the site where our headquarters were located.

19
Getting Ready for Spiritual Armageddon

We had collected invaluable material for lengthy reflections regarding the *miracle of life*, not always valued by human beings when they lack religious faith, ethical and moral values, and commitments to life's realities.

Throughout the week, we visited the family groups that had been invited to help reconstruct the new earth and the happiness of its future inhabitants, as well as those who had willingly committed themselves once they realized that a great revolution of love was happening on the beloved planet.

We returned to the homes of Herminio and Rosalinda, Alonso and Eunice, as well as others, where victorious reincarnations were developing as expected.

The benefactor informed us that, in that gloomy stronghold, where crime had become a constant, and where our Christian Spiritist brothers and sisters were striving to preserve an atmosphere of peace, the messenger that would be reborn in their midst would demonstrate that the environment is not solely responsible for people's behavior; that, due to his evolutionary state, he would stand out in the future, following the beautiful paths of magistracy, so as to modify the grim landscape of the place, completely changing its social, economic and human structure...

On the other hand, Alonso and Eunice's little one would devote himself to the medical sciences in order to make it more humane since it has been undergoing tremendous disrespect by some of its members, who have forgotten the Hippocratic oath in order to make it a profitable industry at the expense of the lives that wither in neglect, far removed from any sense of compassion.

Many others, in whose reincarnation programming we had taken part, would be living ethical lives committed to various areas of scientific and philosophical knowledge, especially politics, where they would serve with dignity, modifying the existing standards of conduct and rendering the constituted laws respectable, starting with themselves.

Realizing this transformation would occur over the entire planet, we could envision a world without borders of hatred and ethnic separatism – always the causes of bloody wars – without economic poverty – bearer of countless evils – and especially without moral poverty, which will vanish, making way for new concepts concerning human behavior. While this transformation has not been fully realized yet – although developing rapidly all over the planet – in the darkness of the lowest realms of the spirit world the enemies of the Good are plotting attacks and hateful revenge against humankind.

Accordingly, bearing in mind that sincere Spiritists are the new Christians – with no disrespect toward the other servants of the Gospel of Jesus scattered throughout the world, or toward other honest citizens not connected to any religious denomination, but who are valiant and upright – the batteries of evil have been set in motion against them. It is also clear that honest individuals with lofty sentiments are not outside the range of the ignominious activities of those unfortunates of the Great Beyond, since they are considered as obstacles to their objectives, that is, the extinction of the Good, subjugations or collective vampirizations – as has always been the case, but now in much greater numbers – along with misadventure and delusion in games of sordid pleasures...

Of course, despite the perverse traps and merciless persecutions, no one is helpless and at the mercy of evil, except when they willingly allow themselves to be connected with these wicked forces...

We will focus specifically on the Spiritist movement committed to Jesus and His doctrine, the primary target of certain groups of the flock self-styled as Evil.

Approaching careless mediums, they have been inspiring behavior that is incompatible with the recommendations of Jesus and the high-order Spirits as stated in the Kardecian Codification,[12] emboldening them to put on spectacles in which mediumship is ridiculed, as if it were an adornment to extol those who possess it. Concomitantly, fostering servile passions in workers dedicated to spiritual assistance at mediumistic meetings, making them believe they are reencountering loved ones from other lifetimes, individuals who are now disturbing their family lives and promoting adulterous behaviors in blatant disregard for moral codes and family responsibilities... Fascination and subjugation, which

---

[12] The Codification consists of five books compiled by Allan Kardec: *The Spirits' Book*, *The Mediums' Book*, *The Gospel according to Spiritism*; *Heaven and Hell*; and *Genesis*. – I.R.

begin subtly and rob many mediums of their discernment, constitute the game of deranged spirits who take advantage of the weaknesses still persisting in human nature...

Besides these nefarious activities, they work for disunity among workers involved in spiritual endeavors, fostering well-publicized slander and defamation, as if they were working for different masters and not for Him who gave His life in an unsurpassed demonstration of love and compassion for all of us.

In certain situations they trigger infirmities difficult to diagnose, concealing their influence on debilitated, weak bodies, leading into the pit of discouragement individuals fond of duty and committed to authentic fraternity.

And when it comes to charity, they goad argumentative people, who waste their time on concepts of paternalism and social inclusion, neglecting to offer real assistance, which consequently arrives too late because time has been wasted on mental idleness and intellectual digression.

The biblical Armageddon of John and the Judeo-Christian traditions is not only restricted to the narrow stretch of the *Valley of Megiddo*, or the hill of the same name, when the armies of all the nations would meet for the final battle...

The entire planet today can be called the *Valley of Jehoshaphat*, where battles of extermination, in which the Lord of mercy will be the victor over imposture and perversity, are already being fought.

Legions of dedicated missionaries of the Good are active everywhere in order to mitigate the consequences of the shortsightedness of some and the despair of others. In the Spiritist Movement, the warnings of Spirit Mentors are continuous but go unheeded by those who are deaf to the truth, inattentive to non-transferable moral renewal, or fickle concerning their commitment. Self-fascinated, they turn into modern Narcissuses...

When the time came, Dr. Santana informed us that a meeting was being scheduled with a former Jewish rabbi, victimized during those terrible days at the end of the 15th century, when non-Catholics were being expelled from Spain.

We were already familiar with the Spiritist Center where our benefactor would be meeting with Eliachim ben Saddoch, who was in command of an impressive band of discarnate criminals currently devoted to a campaign of extermination against the disciples of the Third Revelation.[13]

For us to be successful, Mentors in our sphere of action had already outlined the meeting, for which we would have to be spiritually prepared.

Ready to work and trusting in divine mercy, we headed for the Spiritist Center, where we had previously interned.

The institution devoted to studying the Spiritist Codification in accordance with the strict methods used by Allan Kardec – with emphasis on education in all aspects because it is not only limited to incarnates, but also to suffering discarnates ignorant of the Divine Laws – was in full swing when we arrived.

The study rooms and rooms for treatments involving spiritual fluids and passes[14] were filled with earnest Spiritist volunteer workers and the needy from both planes of life.

---

[13] Adherents of Spiritism. – I.R.
[14] "Passes are a transfusion of energy that alter the cellular field .... In magnetic assistance, emission and reception are entwined, helping needy patients so that they can help themselves." (Andre Luiz, *In the Realms of Mediumship*, Ch. 17, International Spiritist Council, 2011) – I.R.

All the seats in the room reserved for conferences and symposiums, as well as for group passes, were taken by expectant people eager for that evening's enlightened lecture.

The bustle of spirits eager to communicate with family members was impressive, as well as that of individuals tormented by problems of various kinds, having arrived at the Center in the hopes of guidance and comfort for the dramas they bore as inner, hidden crosses.

When the lecturer arrived, we noticed the sincere joy on everyone's faces.

Those who were stressed let go of the marks of their afflictions and externalized vibrations of sympathy that began enveloping the worker of Jesus.

He paused here and there to greet friends and visitors so that everyone had an opportunity to receive the benefit of the energies that he, too, was externalizing.

We accompanied him closely and listened to the spoken and silent requests of a great number of people, who trusted in the inspiration he was about to receive and the blessings they would receive during his message to them.

Ever vigilant, Dr. Santana told us:

"Spiritism is a serious doctrine, which cannot be used for frivolous purposes or for self-promotion by any of its adherents. Representing the *Comforter* promised by Jesus, it is a beautiful, joy-bearing message, not an entertaining spectacle for the frivolous.

"Almost all of these people, as well as the spirits that come here, are tormented by serious issues. They long for balanced guidance and fraternal support in order to recover the strength they need to continue their progress until they are liberated from their physical existence. Family members distressed because of the discarnation of loved ones, sick individuals with various diseases – including severe obsessions – yearn for guidelines of health and peace. Oppressed by socioeconomic and social behavior injunctions, they need kindness and assistance so as not to tumble into the abyss of serious depression, or go mad from the agony of tormenting uncertainties... So obviously, there is no room for hilarity or personal exhibitionism, in a false therapeutic conduct of a circus-like nature...

"There was no one more joyous than Jesus; at the same time, no one could equal His seriousness when dealing with questions concerning the *Kingdom of Heaven*."

Promptly, at the scheduled time, respectful of everyone's commitments, the Center's director began the meeting by inviting everyone to join him in a prayer of thanksgiving and requesting inspiration for that evening's endeavors.

As he prayed fervently, he was haloed by a delicate light that radiated outward.

When he finished, he gave the floor to the person in charge of the lecture, who addressed the *Parable of the Prodigal Son*, carefully reading the text and then interpreting it in terms compatible with current psychological, philosophical, ethical, sociological, and especially, Spiritist knowledge...

New angles were covered; hidden subtleties in the lessons were exposed; the teachings were made current – all in accurate language and in colloquial tones, leading the attentive listeners to inner reflections that would help them understand the deeper meaning of Jesus' message.

Interweaving the lecture with humorous remarks now and then in a healthy teaching methodology that did not diminish the seriousness of the content inspired by a noble scholar on our plane, he touched us all with his enlightening and kindly words.

When he finished, the psychosphere was one of peace, opening space for group passes as the mediums took their various positions, initiating the vibrations that conveyed to everyone present the reinvigorating energies that the mediums were absorbing and distributing, illuminating the entire place.

Discarnate family members approached and inspired their loved ones while the latter prayed fervently, and after the closing prayer, everyone left filled with ineffable well-being and inwardly renewed for the challenges of evolution.

Afterward, the lecturer went into a small adjoining room, where he continued his service by listening to and counseling people that had been previously selected by the fraternal attendants.

Always accompanied by selfless messengers from our plane under the guidance of his mentor, he offered the spiritual nourishment of the word of the Gospel with Spiritist explanations concerning each one's problems, while the spirit benefactors made note of the address of each patient in order to continue helping him or her with their resources.

Order, discipline and cleanliness of the entire institution were present everywhere, demonstrating that serving the Good should not be carelessly improvised, but deserved the respect given to all important issues.

After a few hours of fraternal assistance, the director went home with some friends that helped him at the Center. We stayed behind, taking part in the activities in our sphere of action.

Although the facilities were closed on the physical plane, Spiritist lectures continued in the room, while in the other parts, devoted spirits continued helping the needy of every kind.

Work is the tonic that keeps everything in balance everywhere.

Rest is an organic need, but too much of it leads to the avoidance of responsibilities under false pretenses. A change in activity, awakening new emotional stimuli, also serves to renew one's energies.

The night wore on when the workers specializing in the kind of meeting that would soon take place arrived.

In the mediumistic room specially reserved for disobsession, the activity of spirits dedicated to that task was significant. One endeavor had just ended, and technicians specialized in environmental psychic cleansing came into the room to prepare it for the next one.

20
Confrontation with the Darkness

The members, who were selected from among the incarnates, were trained to help spirits obstinate in evil, so they were used to the arguments that always take place during such specialized assistance.

The medium Joseval, who had been responsible for that evening's lecture, had been brought there by his mentor. He displayed significant lucidity, accustomed as he was to working in partial disengagement during physiological sleep and in the spiritual endeavors in our sphere.

Cheerful, he welcomed us all, showing special affection towards this humble narrator. He placed himself entirely at the disposal of Dr. Santana, who would be supervising the scheduled activity.

One of the guards stationed at the institution's entrance approached to notify us that the group of Jewish rabbis was approaching, putting on a pompous show with extravagant costumes. The high priest Eliachim ben Saddoch was in the lead, walking proudly with a grimace of hatred and arrogance on his face. He was accompanied by over a hundred other chieftains, also wearing fearsome expressions, some with visible deformities. They stopped at the main entry.

Trained *dogs*, which seemed to have been human beings at one time, but were now hypnotized, assuming animalistic forms as a result of their cruelty during previous existences, prevented a large number of followers and victims of the leaders of the sad cohort from causing any embarrassment.

When they reached the area bordering the front entry, they assumed a preposterous, medieval-looking fighting stance, wielding strange instruments of war. Clamoring wildly, they seemed to be waiting for orders.

A venerable female spirit approached the arrogant leader and disarmed him with the simplicity of her garments and her emanation of compassion and tenderness. She invited him to enter the room, where he was being awaited with respect and affection. A few members of his strange and gloomy entourage were also invited in...

He was carrying a voluminous number of yellowed and worn scrolls, which he handed to one of his assistants and then followed the gracious hostess. Ten other priests of ancient sects derived from Judaism in Europe were also let into the room, while the other members of the strange caravan and the pack of desperate servants and underlings remained behind, furious and agitated.

In the meantime, the spirit director prayed:

Lord Jesus, August Master:
Although the darkness of ignorance prevails in our inner world, let the sublime light of Your ineffable love flood us with light, freeing us from our persistent, domineering wickedness.

We are no other spirits but reprobates who have denied you more than once, albeit members in the ranks of Your Gospel, assuming pernicious debts that still put us to shame.

> *Today, once again called by Your mercy to do illuminative work, we acknowledge our frailty; thus we let ourselves be guided by Your holy hands, following the luminous footprints of Your passage on the earth...*
>
> *So help us to help others, rescuing those who were our victims when we defrauded Your message, wretched as we were because of the sordid interests of our pettiness.*
>
> *Make our words smooth and energetic, our sentiments lofty and gentle, our mind lucid and understanding so that we do not hinder the fulfillment of Your plans for the unfortunate, who are nearly all of us.*
>
> *With a new dawn breaking, provide us with the unusual happiness of broadening our still-dark horizons into the light of Your truth.*
>
> *The brother we are about to receive, along with others who have fallen into the deep abyss of hatred, still remember what we did to them in the past, when we defiled Your name with our passions.*
>
> *Have mercy on us all, Your most humble servants, and be with us from this time on through Your sublime messengers so that we may best contribute to Your fruitful harvest.*
>
> *So be it!*

When he finished, he showed the emotion that had taken all of us.

An indescribable wave of peace overwhelmed us and we were united in a gentle harmony of tenderness.

When we reached the room, duly protected by fluidic currents carefully distributed around the building and, in particular, the mediumistic room, the wrathful challenger could not hide his displeasure. He had expected more consideration and homage, which obviously could not be given.

"Welcome to the House of Jesus," Dr. Santana greeted him purposely, showing respect and friendship.

"Do not speak that name to me," the other responded, totally put-off. "I do not have the slightest consideration for that nefarious, mythological creature of the tradition of the rulers of the earth."

And he laughed boisterously.

Although all of the newcomers reacted with blasphemies, Dr. Santana approached the medium Joseval, who was in semi-trance, and before the high priest even realized it, he was drawn into Joseval's perispiritual field like iron filings to a magnet.

The medium, in a troubled trance, assumed an arrogant attitude while the spirit shouted:

"We have fallen into a trap typical of nefarious Christians of all times. Advance and attack these miserable traitors right now!"

The other guests could barely move because the environmental energies kept them from acting according to their established plans. They remained immobilized by the vibrations all of us were directing towards them.

In light of this impossibility, they began to scream in pitiful desperation, hoping to be heard by their minions outside expecting an open-air battle.

Dr. Santana remained calm, and after a brief moment amid the priest's and his companions' accusations, he answered with irreprehensible benevolence:

"Your claim that we betrayed you and led you into a trap is unjustified, because the challenge came from you, my distinguished friend, a challenge we accepted for a meeting of clarification, not a battle characteristic of the biblical Armageddon, as you would wish, in a plan of revenge and war."

"I won't stay here," the other reacted ferociously, squirming in the mediumistic trance, "and listen to your familiar rants. I have been the victim of the deceitful arguments of infamous Christians more than once... Let's get out of here. Oftentimes, retreat is the best strategy in combat, especially when the troops are victims of the villainy and sordidness of an enemy that has lured them into a filthy trap. Christians will never be worthy of facing the truth found in the Torah and in the false words of that justly punished enemy of Israel."

"I can assure you – my friend and brother – that we mean you no harm. Accepting your offer concerning the battle that has endured the night of several centuries, ours is the desire for fraternity and peace. We acknowledge your power in the infernal regions, where you hide out with other spirits who were vilely deceived and betrayed in the past, when we were still dominated by the ferocity of the lower passions. Time has run in the hourglass and we have all changed, for the better, I believe, because the clear message of Jesus has finally reached the landscapes of our minds and the country of our sentiments.

"We beseech your sincere forgiveness, as well as that of all those whom we harmed. We acknowledge our lamentable wrong and its awful consequences. We are truly repentant and we wish to demonstrate our moral transformation by welcoming you and all those who have longed for peace, which they haven't enjoyed for such a long time, a peace that only Jesus can give."

"Do not speak that name anymore!" he responded in a rage.

"I am sorry but I cannot comply. The servant is not greater than the master, nor the slave better than his lord. Jesus is our Way, our Hope for total liberation, our safe harbor."

"If he was all of that," the other grumbled ironically, "I would not be here, constrained and unable to do what I please. It only confirms my distrust of him and the scum who follow him."

Dr. Santana replied patiently, "It just so happens that you came here with plans for a fight, using the weapons of resentment and revenge, propelled by others of a destructive character, such as you use in your realm."

"That war rages on," the other fought back, with eyes bulging out of their sockets, exposing the face behind the mask, "and we shall defeat our enemies. We shall not allow the pernicious doctrine now reborn in Spiritism to spread – that poisonous legacy of the cursed Christianity of priests and princes of the fraudulent church."

"Indeed," answered the noble enlightener, "Spiritism shines in the heavens of the planet, confirming Jesus' promise that he would not leave us as orphans. His love and compassion have enabled the pages He wrote in the sanctuary of nature to be read through sublime words and unparalleled examples, but which we adulterated, adapting them to our own miserable interests, giving way to a doctrine far removed from authenticity. But since it is never too late to start over, to retrace one's steps and correct mistakes, we are committed to rehabilitation."

"Words and more words that will neither alter the ignoble acts of the past, nor alter our plans for revenge," exploded the other.

Lifting the medium up in a threatening posture, he asked with unbridled hostility:

"Just look at the unhappy landscape of the earth. Where are the so-much-praised meekness and prudence, compassion and mercy? Do you not see, perchance, what is happening on that world rich in illusory powers and degradation? Where are the disciples of the Crucified One hiding, that bearer of much guilt, who duped them all with his empty words and promises?"

"Yes, we see the presence of the light where darkness used to reign; love where hatred used to sow destruction; tenderness instead of aggressiveness, and the work of rebuilding on the rubble of the deceitful glories of the past. A new era has been foretold, when suffering will give way to the joy of living, and when the deadened sentiments will foster the flourishing of the high ideals of human dignity. It is just a matter of time before the present, unfortunate situation will be resolved, for the time has come when the earth and its inhabitants will be constrained to reach higher levels of evolution."

"When the children of Alcyone take over and expel the earthlings?" the other asked sarcastically.

"It's not like that at all. We are receiving visitors from another dimension, who intend to help us with the transformations that are already taking place on the planet, because the Law that prevails in the universe is that of harmony, solidarity and the moral principles established by the Father Creator."

A horrifying laugh thundered through the deformed lips of the communicating spirit, now manifesting himself in all his beastly, lycanthropic hideousness.

The medium crouched over and howled like a wolf. A foul odor permeated the environment as the former rabbi's followers underwent equivalent modifications.

We began breathing a very dense, heavy, almost suffocating psychosphere.

Meanwhile, filled with compassion and sincerely touched by the dolorous spectacle, the fervently praying members of the meeting slowly began generating vibrations that diluted the dense psychic mist, and, unexpectedly and convulsing, the spirit hissed:

"Nothing will stop me now... We shall meet again... elsewhere, you despicable coward."

"Yes," responded our benefactor, "we will meet in your stronghold."

As if torn violently away, he detached himself from the perispirit of the medium, who would have fallen to the floor if Dr. Santana had not been alert, supporting him and sitting him upright.

The other spirits with him were drawn into the same vibratory wave and the room gradually returned to its initial harmony.

Revealing his joy, our mentor explained to us:

"That reaction was anticipated because, in reality, that was not the former rabbi Eliachim ben Saddoch, but a clone, a spirit who assimilated his characteristics in order to deceive us. From his stronghold he followed every move of our meeting.

"Skillful and cunning, he did not want to risk a direct confrontation. First, he sent from his kingdom of horror simulators strongly linked to his powerful mind, which then pulled them from our premises – with the permission of our Guides, of course – so that we would not discover the ruse. Since violence is unnecessary in our work, and it was not for us to prevent our visitors from leaving, measures were taken for the dialogue to continue only as long as necessary for the metamorphoses to occur, dissolving the *fluidic masks* they used to hide their true identity.

"Deceivers always fool and delude themselves while they believe they are deceiving others.

"We consider the task successful under the blessings of Jesus, and it will have its natural continuation at the right time in the future.

"Let us continue our blessed endeavor."

With everyone's concentration renewed, we watched as sister Arlinda, a venerable worker with more than half a century of dedication to the Cause of the Good, went into a trance and began to emit energy in the form of ectoplasm through her facial orifices. A high order spirit took shape, bathed in bluish light, and condensed in the room saturated with fragrant, lofty vibrations.

He immediately identified himself as an ambassador of Ishmael, Brazil's spirit guide, bringing the support of that noble mentor:

> *Dear brothers and sisters:*
> *May Jesus keep us in his peace and mercy.*
> *Your prayers have reached the blessed realms, and the angel benefactor of Brazil has sent us so that you may receive his honorable support in your blessed endeavor.*
> *The homeland of the Cross will play its Christian role on the troubled world scene of today.*

Missionaries of love and of the liberation of consciences have been reborn among you with the task of returning to the world the glorious message of the gentle, kind Galilean Rabbi, a message that has suffered the changes foreseen for centuries.

Committed to Truth, they have the task of living what they teach, shaping the metals of the soul so they will conform to their new purposes.

Although the paths are still covered with thorns, and obstacles make progress slow everywhere, these pilgrims of duty are forged of courage and fearlessness, never held back but always advancing.

Missionary spirits of bygone eras, accustomed to austerity and renunciation, inspire us to succeed.

Misunderstood and slandered, suffering scorn and facing colossal challenges, they advance, confident in the happy result of the endeavor they have been committed to since before their birth.

Their vibrant word and their worthy examples convince those who hear them and those familiar with them that we are indeed on the threshold of a new era of love, peace and truth.

No more the hoaxes of yesteryear, nor the cajolery of the misguided journey to the realm of illusion.

Seriousness and sacrifice are the badges of honor they wear on the garments of the soul, identifying them as followers of Jesus, who had no other choice between the deceitful glory of the earth and the liberating cross that led him back to immortality in triumph.

They travel the same paths as in the past, on which they left footprints marked by crimes and vices, footprints which they must now erase by superposing the luminous purposes of pure love and undisguised truth.

Psychically connected to our Sphere, they receive constant encouragement so as not to faint in tough battles, nor stray from their course, animated by the spirit of joy and the reward of inner peace.

Persecuted by the enemies of the Light, they have equipped themselves with the instruments of defense – prayer and ennobled acts.

Even as the great Brazilian nation plunges into the depths of debauchery, corruption, and disrespect for the codes of justice and honesty – a passing phase in its evolution – compassionate Ishmael intercedes before Jesus on behalf of all, believing in the changes that are already occurring with a new generation of men and women of the Good.

Of course, the same applies to the various countries of the earth; however by determination of the incomparable Master, the task of returning to the world His message of mercy and complete deliverance has fallen to Brazil.

Strive, therefore, in the objectives you have embraced. Never fear the forces of evil, which dissolve like mist in the heat of the sun of truth, implementing the era of love as essential for the happiness of all.

You have been the object of traps and betrayals, of testimonies you keep in silence, never retaliating against evil, always realizing that you are disciples of the One who did not defend Himself against the undue charges leveled at Him, thus being the model for you to follow.

Loneliness, contempt, and inner suffering because of unfulfilled longings are injunctions resulting from your behavior in past reincarnations.

Keep today the brightness of joy and goodness on your face and in your sentiments, creating harmony wherever you go.

You will never experience abandonment, nor will you suffer the absence of your loving spirit guides. They will be with you until the completion of your task, when you return to the great spiritual homeland.

May the Lord bless you and keep you always,
Your brother and servant,
Bittencourt Sampaio

As we wiped away the tears, the luminous figure of the spirit ambassador of Ishmael dissolved, leaving fluidic breezes of peculiar well-being that effusively penetrated all of us.

Slowly, the medium regained lucidity, conscious that she had been the instrument used in the materialization of a special messenger. She thanked the Lord for his blessing in heartfelt prayer.

As for me, I could not contain the emotions that followed in a kaleidoscope of fond memories of my last existence on earth, when I had the opportunity to read works written by the venerable mentor Bittencourt Sampaio, a former president of the Brazilian Spiritist Federation.

When the time came to end the activities, Dr. Santana informed the director, who prayed movingly, and then said goodbye to all of us until the next opportunity.

The smiling face of the sun had not yet appeared, but its strands of light were already drawing signs in the darkness that had engulfed the night.

21
Difficult Battles

Our conversations after the memorable meeting addressed the issue of the deceitfulness of certain low-order spirits. Taken by surprise at the unmasking of the malevolent visitor, I asked the enlightened director of our work:

"How dare those fellows try such a thing at a meeting of such high magnitude as that in which we were fortunate enough to participate? Also, about the dissolution of the mask used by that wretched spirit to conceal his true identity: how did that occur?"

Our benefactor, always expecting our questions, explained:

"Ignorance is the inspirer of cunning, which tries to conceal itself, incurring regrettable mistakes.

"Rabbi Saddoch prepared the disguise with the intent of misleading us. He used ideoplasty to create his minion's guise by means of hypnosis, together with his underling's mental self-fixation to reproduce his, Rabbi Saddoch's, image and let it mold the other's features. With this resource, his ambassador was prepared for the task, allying the arrogance peculiar to the wretched with the hypocrisy Rabbi Saddoch is accustomed to in the den were he takes refuge.

"During the trance, the medium's healthy energies helped dissolve the disguise. At the same time, the underling's rage restored him to the normal, lycanthropic condition to which he had adapted over the centuries as his temporary reality.

"We realized what was going on right away due to his vibratory emanations, in addition to his weak argumentation. We often find ourselves in these minefield-like situations, where caution is necessary for the sake of compassion and truth.

"Thus, we focused on his neuralgic point, the thing that would upset him the most, which was the name of Jesus Christ, causing him the emotional distress and imbalance we witnessed.

"We must never forget that, for the messengers of evil and those who behave badly, everything is valid as long as it corresponds to their goals. They do not follow commendable methods because, treading the narrow paths of madness, they are unable to decide between what is ethical and what is not."

"Because of what happened," I asked, "should our work continue in the caves of the planet's entrails, where he dwells and maintains his sad empire of madness?"

Always prepared to educate and instruct, he replied:

"Considering the robustness of the empire of darkness and turpitude, an incursion into his den would be neither easy nor prudent for now. Let us remember that since the end of the 15th century he has been working with other reprobates to wreak revenge on those who hurt him, transferring responsibility to the Martyr of Galilee. It is an actual State, with all the mechanisms needed to support his policy of hatred. It has an administrative organization in a community inhabited by hundreds of thousands of reprobates, some by their own will, others taken there compulsorily and subjected to unspeakable sufferings, as occurs in barbaric cultures under the command of heartless despots.

"We mustn't violate the codes of love, for even though our wills are imbued with the best intentions, they are not above the Sovereign Laws of Justice and Mercy, from which no one escapes...

"We need to wait a few more days in order to evaluate the effect of our first direct contact with the rabbi through his misguided clone.

"Let us remember that this effort is to be considered highly important in view of the moral revolution currently taking place on this planet of transition.

"Our brothers and sisters will intensify their assaults on the servants of the Master, as well as against society in general, aiming to win victories of folly and horror. Generating mental and emotional disorders, and encouraging people's lower tendencies, they hope for responses in the form of ever-increasing moral disarray, culminating in domestic, urban, national and even international violence through calamitous wars.

"They forget that progress is unavoidable and that evil is ephemeral. In their delusion they have lost the ability to reason with discernment, seeing nothing beyond their defiant activities and their relentless pursuit to round up new followers as victims or sympathizers...

"Our goal is to decrease the effects of such crude behavior on the social organism, releasing those who have fallen into the webs of obsession due to through foolishness and carelessness, thus decreasing the evils taking place in contemporary society.

"The ultimate determination is in the hands of the terrestrial ship's Captain, our Master and Lord."

There was no time for any more questions, since other duties required his presence.

We remained in our activity center, and since we had not yet been called to new commitments, Lopes Neto, Ivon, some other friends and myself decided to visit a few institutions dedicated to the Good – some public, some governmental, and others non-governmental – in order to learn from other companions devoted to lessons of good service.

We first chose a public emergency hospital and could not hide our dismay at the number of the sick and the suffering, as well as the indifference with which they were treated. The room was full, as was the unkempt corridor, where the disregard for human life and the aggressiveness of some staff – paid to provide good service – predominated.

Disrespected concerning their right to support and care, the patients were writhing in all kinds of pain, fighting for a spot to see the doctor, who was usually cross, perhaps due to being exhausted or overwhelmed, showing a lack of ethics and compassion for others.

Of course he could not attend to all of them at the same time. Nonetheless kindness, patience and mercy toward the afflicted were still possible.

The interaction between incarnates and discarnates was frightening. The majority of patients displayed dreadful pictures of spirit-related disturbances to varying degrees of gravity, from simple obsessions to subjugations and unrelenting vampirizations.

Our attention was called to a gentleman of about sixty, sitting in a wheelchair in the narrow corridor, bathed in algid sweat. He had serious heart problems and his wife was pleading for emergency care. The ill-willed staff member stated that the doctor had not yet arrived and that there was no other recourse but to seek relief in another hospital...

Deepening our observation, we found that, beside the heart disease reflected in every trait of the patient, a ferocious spirit had bound him with *metallic chains* that compressed his chest while he tried to asphyxiate him. The avenger sought to hypnotize the patient with his gaze, mentally suggesting suicide as the solution.

The man was in agony, powerless to fight back, his mind in complete disarray. He suddenly fainted, and panic set in with screams that someone was dying and needed help.

A nurse rushed to his aid and massaged his heart area, while his horror-inspiring discarnate enemy exulted gleefully.

In agony, the woman who was pushing his wheelchair began to plead for divine assistance. We had no choice but to approach him, and while Lopes Neto raised his thought in a moving intercessory prayer, Ivon Costa began applying bio-energies, first to release the morbiferous fluids asphyxiating him, and then to transmit vitality to him.

Slowly coming out of the faint, bathed in sweat and with an expression of horror on his face, the patient was rushed to the ICU, while chaos still reigned among the others.

We accompanied him and noticed that the wicked avenger had momentarily lost control over his victim due to Ivon's beneficent energies.

Nonetheless he remained watchful, waiting. We contacted him mentally and he exploded in bitter complaint:

"As incredible as it may seem," he harangued, almost insane, "this is my only son, if I can call him that. I was a man of some means. An asthma sufferer since childhood, some thirty years ago during one of my worst attacks the wretch decided to seize my assets. While I was suffering an attack of dyspnea, he smothered me with a pillow. No one saw him do it. Afterward he positioned my body to look like I had suffocated in my sleep.

"There was no suspicion, because my old ailment was well-known.

"I couldn't believe it and went crazy at the terrible phony scene the next day. During my burial, while I ranted, he pretended to weep, mourning the death of his dear old dad.

"I swore revenge on the wretch, which I had been pursuing judiciously for five years, when his heart problem appeared, perhaps caused by his remorse and perversity.

"I won't give him a moment's peace until I see him here beside me, when we will settle accounts."

Touched by the tragedy, Ivon attempted a dialogue, but the discarnate was not interested. He remained at his son's side, like the serpent that hypnotizes its victim before striking.

When healthcare workers finally understand the serious commitment they have assumed regarding their sick brothers and sisters, awakening to spiritual reality and connecting to prayer, charity and inspiration, hospitals will be transformed into temples of mercy and comprehensive health...

In that chaos, we also observed the sacrificial work of many high-order spirits and discarnate doctors and nurses, as well as the patients' family and friends trying to reduce the serious damage resulting from government mismanagement and the neglect of a few ill-humored staff.

We saw that we could not do anything more for now, and after following several other appalling cases of unfortunate exchange between the incarnate and discarnate populations, we headed for a home for girls, run by an NGO that enjoyed an upstanding ethical reputation in the city.

We had no trouble finding the well-designed institution. It was a spacious and clean building that housed children who did not know their parents.

It was home to eighty girls whose ages varied from a few months to nineteen years.

The very clean nursery contained a dozen little ones. They had eaten and were now asleep, being watched over by one of the staff.

Others were playing out in the large, tree-lined courtyard, while still others were involved in domestic chores, helping in the kitchen and pantry, as well as taking care of their belongings.

The director was a widow approximately fifty-five years old, cheerful and energetic, bearer of excellent vibrations, friendly and sincerely devoted to her work, for which she received no pay at all.

A Catholic, she devoted her work to St. Therese of Jesus so that it could be forwarded to the Lord, and she sought to infuse all who served in the institution with the sentiments of kindness, courtesy and love toward children and toward each other.

Several discarnate mothers watched over the girls in an effort to assist the devoted staff, while others, still dazed and confused, did not understand what had happened to them, but were aware of the presence of their little ones.

Good and industrious spirits contributed to everyone's welfare in a climate of high vibrations, maintaining the harmony and joy of living expressed among those who lived and worked there. The happy result was that the work was successful, enriching and full of emotional rewards.

The visit went very well because it showed that the first step to the victory of the Good is the moral transformation of the human being for the better, overcoming *bad inclinations* and adopting healthy behaviors.

The great, serious battle is always fought on the inner landscapes of each individual for the installation of love and truth in the heart. It is not an easy struggle in that we are heirs to vices and excesses that lasted through the millennia up until it was possible for us to awaken to renewing, positive emotions, which must prevail over primitive passions.

People have always been preoccupied with winning a victory over others, over those they think are their enemies, whereas the true enemies are hidden or unveiled in the dark corners of their own soul.

It was for no other reason that Jesus stressed individual responsibility when people are informed of their immortality and the authentic values that dignify and liberate the conscience.

In turn, Spiritism came to awaken individuals to a life of noble postulates, which are presented as traditional virtues, magnified by achievements of behavioral and moral elevation.

Thus self-examination is a non-transferable duty for all those who want to make order and harmony among the earth's people a reality, so much so that we are prepared not to give shelter to the intuitions of evil, represented by old tendencies, primeval feelings, and the terrible villains, descendants of the ego, the children of fear, anger and its minions.

Renewed and joyful, we headed for other spirits dedicated to the Good. Our first visit was to a nursing home run by disciples of *the Comforter*.

It was a wooded area on the outskirts of the city. Two buildings had been built there, each with two floors and several areas of manicured gardens with corners adorned with painted iron benches used for fraternal socializing among the residents.

One of the buildings was completely devoted to small, comfortable apartments for men or women, avoiding any kind of segregation and using the conventional family nucleus as the reference.

Two apartments were connected by a bathroom between them for the residents' convenience. Two neat beds composed the simple bedroom, and beside each bed was a small table for personal belongings, pictures of loved ones, books, etc.

The patients, some very old and senile, in addition to having heartbreaking illnesses, were treated with warmth and kindness.

There were daily studies of *The Gospel according Spiritism* by Allan Kardec, where the important topic of death was examined carefully, with neither threat of punishment, nor promise of undeserved privileges in the afterlife. Everything was done with great simplicity, but with fraternal affection, attesting to the consciousness of a job well done.

A number of delirious patients were screaming or blaspheming, laughing or showing agitation under the supervision of the physician on duty, the staff and the spirit benefactors that toiled there.

We were welcomed by brother Aurelio. Aurelio was in charge of the work, for he had been its founder more than fifty years ago. We had the immense joy of visiting all the departments, listening to Aurelio's explanations.

Taking note of our interest in getting to know some of the charitable endeavors in order to expand our learning, Aurelio showed us a place of love dedicated to the repose of patients discharged from hospitals. They had been without assistance in the difficult period of convalescence, especially those that had come from inland cities for surgical treatments.

After receiving directions we headed for the blessed home, a modern building with three floors and several departments that offered care to sufferers as well as lessons in Spiritism.

We were greeted at the entrance by a venerable benefactor of humanity,[15] who had left behind on the earth a remarkable work in the lands of the former French Equatorial Africa, and who also worked in this place of love.

Surprised by his presence, the wise friend perceived our perplexity and explained that love has no homeland.

---

[15] We can safely assume that this benefactor was "Albert Schweitzer (1875-1965), 1952 Nobel Peace Prize; Only nine when he first performed in his father's church, he was, from his young manhood to his middle eighties, recognized as a concert organist, internationally known. From his professional engagements he earned funds for his education, particularly his later medical schooling, and for his African hospital." www.nobelprize.org. – I.R.

"As a young man I was a talented classical organist, but I did not hesitate to leave the beautiful landscapes of my birthplace for the stifling climate of the African forests in the name of Jesus' love for His unfortunate brothers and sisters. After discarnation, because I was attracted by the love of the founders of this home, a couple completely dedicated to the Good in its sublime expression of charity, I agreed to participate in the beautiful ideal of service to the needy."

He led us to the various rooms, especially the infirmaries/dormitories, where we found women and men recovering from surgery, while others, who used to live on the streets, found support to help them recover and return to social life.

Coincidentally, at that very moment the founders appeared: the selfless couple, servants of Jesus, tireless workers of beneficence.

The wife was surrounded by a delicate filigree of light, demonstrating great mediumistic sensitivity, while the husband, equally confident in the Good, spoke about the needs of the place, which at the time was experiencing some economic difficulties, an issue that did not disturb its program, however.

Visiting the sick, we noticed that some maintained their connection with spirit adversaries, from whom they were starting to break free due to the Spiritist therapies used there, including passes, energized water, Gospel-based psychotherapies, and disobsession meetings held at the Spiritist Center's own site.

Friends from both spheres of life met alongside volunteers who offered to help the patients until they were able to go home. Some of their family members, staying in modest lodgings nearby, also visited them, grateful and filled with holy vibrations of peace.

When our tour was finished, we thanked the kind spirit and headed for yet other assistance institutions, acquiring the experience necessary for the work of self-enlightenment, often witnessing the lack of interest of regular human beings occupied with their own needs, as well as by the powerful of the world, many of whom were completely divorced from the solidarity that should reign in all hearts.

We also spent some time in the dens of drug addiction in city squares, public gardens and back alleys, where children were using crack, some already showing the symptoms of brain disorders in tandem with behavioral problems.

The always agonizing human landscape awakened our sentiments of compassion and mercy, leading us to intercessory prayer for all controlled by addictions, those that had fallen into the traps of the evil they had committed against themselves in other lifetimes, when they indulged in lust, pride and crime – whether legalized or not – and now caught in the powerful webs of urgent repair through suffering.

The hours passed by quickly, and after having spent such useful time with the sowers of the Good, we returned to the Spiritist Center where we were staying.

22
Preparations for the Conclusion of Our Work

That night was especially splendid, speckled with a myriad of stars, like sparkling diamonds encased in the festive dome.

The longings of nature were wafting by, borne in the arms of a light breeze filled with fragrance. It was springtime in the region, and the ground, covered with soft grass and delicate plants, exulted before the blessings of life.

Our benefactor, who displayed special joy, explained that a review of our labors over the previous three months was needed, from our first foray into the desolate region of Sumatra, to when we and others returned to the beloved planet for endeavors concerning reincarnations during the period of the great transition, culminating with our experiences alongside deeply misguided brothers and sisters in the grips of evil.

Other labors scheduled for the most miserable areas, those that harbored rebellious spirits hardened in cruelty, would be set aside until the appropriate time, when guidelines would be established for that purpose. Among these would be a carefully planned visit to the infernal region, home to Rabbi Eliachim ben Saddoch and his misguided subjects... The never-ending work of the Good would continue in other areas, contributing to the progress of society and the beloved planet.

After his usual instructions, we started our journey of visiting some of the many couples that had volunteered for the reincarnations of the guests from Alcyone, as well as the illustrious missionaries from the past now returning to the earth. The last phase would be a visit to the Spiritist Center where we had stayed on another occasion in order to fulfill our commitment in that stronghold of love and charity, where countless blessings were lavished on everyone.

It is obvious that the reincarnation program also entailed normal reincarnations, wherein spirits were returning under better conditions to be able to participate in the new project of illuminating lives, thus hastening the transition.

Millions of highly accomplished terrestrial spirits were marked to further their tasks – as I mentioned earlier – reincarnating during this wonderful period of renewal and hope.

All, of course, would be under the special care of those in charge of the New Era so that no one would suffer any impediment, as long as they were focused on relevant commitments and maintained the purposes of inner growth.

There has never ever been a spiritual revolution of such magnitude, compared to the significance of these grand moments of human spiritual evolution.

The joy of those responsible for reincarnations, who, in one way or another received our assistance, was immense.

Visiting them and talking with them while partially disengaged during physiological sleep, we shared in their emotions and their desires so that they could soon have their beloved little ones in their lap, working with them on projects involving the new earth, the world of promise...

At such times they expressed their emotions as tears of joy and gratitude to God due to the importance of their willingly accepted commitment.

The sublime award of parenthood for all had a very special meaning because it fostered the development of emotions that derive from co-creation alongside the Exalted Creator.

In their turn, those reincarnating were doing their utmost to measure up to their responsibilities.

Any light in the darkness and morass is noticed, attracting to its epicenter all those who linger in the dark. In one way or another they would be the new bearers of standards of moral and spiritual behavior, meeting the serious challenges and disruptions set in motion to hinder their progress.

This phenomenon always happens as a result of the rebelliousness of the insensate before the serenity of the bearers of existential meaning, which does not end with the grave. In every age, the good and upright have been denounced, misunderstood and persecuted, suffering the sarcasm and the repudiation of those who take pleasure in their own abominable situations.

But they shall never lack the resources originated in the spirit world whence we have all come, so that grand endeavors may be crowned with success.

We continued to witness the descent of the *fascicles of light* toward the terrestrial globe, representing the tutelary beings that entered the planet's atmosphere to carry out their glorious task.

We also made note of the voluminous waves of horror and suffering that crushed entire communities, choking the ideals of many and razing all constructions whose foundations were not firmly set on solid rock – according to Jesus' powerful expression.

In some ways this fight is very old in that there have always been good and bad spirits on the earth, those who have chosen progress as life's norm, and those who have opted for different paths, resulting in distressing and harrowing re-beginnings...

We were in the place chosen for the closure of our excursion, when Dr. Santana was approached by one of the discarnate members of the beloved Center.

Displaying serious apprehension on his face, he requested help for one of the institution's mediums who was in a very serious predicament.

He quickly explained the problem.

It was an armed robbery involving one of Jesus' workers, threatened with death by a heavily drugged criminal.

The victim had prayed for the help of his mentors, and his prayer was heard by us.

Without further ado, the benefactor invited us to accompany the intermediary of the request, and we headed for an awful street set in dense darkness due to the deleterious fluids imbuing the region dedicated to the trade in human flesh...

The robber had demanded the victim to hand over his watch, cell phone and money, and was trying to decide whether to kill him or not, when we arrived. The gun wavered in his trembling hand, his finger on the trigger.

Controlled by his terrible obsessor, the young addict was receiving his adversary's cruel inspiration to go ahead and shoot his helpless target.

At that moment Dr. Santana sent his thought toward the cruel discarnate and admonished him, informing him that he would be liable for the lives of both murderer and victim, and that the heinous crime would be added to his nefarious curriculum.

He sternly touched the forehead of the assailant under the obsessor's grip, stopping the flow of disgraceful inspiration, while at the same time influencing him to abandon the robbery altogether.

Dr. Santana's energy discharges reached his crown and brow chakras, producing a momentary release from his cold and merciless adversary. Next he sent a new wave of powerful energy into his heart center, which had a profound emotional effect, causing him to drop the revolver and collapse from arterial hypotension.

Evandro, the stunned medium, perceived the selfless benefactor's interference and recovered from the shock. He picked up his belongings and, tele-guided by the guide, he quickly left the dark region.

Dominated by different emotions, Evandro began to remember that the reason that had brought him there was a Christian objective: charity to a young woman now living the last moments of her tormented earthly existence, lying on a miserable cot in a flea-infested shack where, in the past, she would sell her feeble body...

It was not the first time he had visited her since being informed of the degradation of her existence. He had taken her food and money to help her support her fragile and defeated body, while the angel of death circled her days of suffering.

Tears flowed from his half-open eyes. We could read his compassionate thoughts, but inspired by the gentle mentor, he decided to return home.

Working for the Good in today's tumultuous world is still a major challenge. Nonetheless those practicing charity and doing good should not get discouraged, for if there are obsessors in the afterlife, always willing to commit heinous crimes, there are also swarms of tutelary angels, vigilant and swift, carrying out labors of true fraternity.

Shortly afterward, an uproar engulfed the sordid stronghold, when someone saw the young man who had passed out. He was coming to, broken and under the effect of his drug addiction and the vibratory shock he had experienced.

Since he was known in the area, the matter was closed after a few disparaging comments. The locale returned to its condition as a dark stronghold of crime and vulgarity.

Our new task completed, we returned to the Spiritist Center, where we were greeted by Dr. Santana and several coworkers, including Evandro's spirit guide.

The night wore on and the streets were slowly becoming deserted.

The sanctuary that welcomed us was enveloped in a sapphire-blue light that flooded every corner. Discarnate workers were present because they had been informed of the closure of our current activities. There were also several mediums and friends of Jesus in partial disengagement during physiological sleep, all there to take part in the farewells...

We were led to the conference and study hall, which was packed. The Center's loving guide invited our benefactor to sit at the head table. We were shown to the reserved seats at the front and the rest of the guests sat in the seats reserved for them. A mezzanine in the back, prepared with spiritual energies, was also completely filled.

In the natural silence, we heard a soft melody that seemed to come from an unknown region of the spirit world. The melody was enriched with children's voices, extolling life and love, while delicate flakes of some luminous substance fell in abundance upon all gathered in silent prayer.

When the melody finally faded away, Joaquina stood and prayed emotionally, beseeching Jesus' blessings on the meeting and asking for His sublime presence to vitalize us, needy as we were for help and wisdom.

The mediums seated close to us concentrated and began to externalize energy similar to ectoplasm, which was directed to a transparent tube on the platform where the head table was located.

The vapor slowly entered the cylinder and began to form a human figure, which, to our utter joy, was Dr. Artemio Guimarães.

When he finished materializing, he exited the tube and approached the podium, externalizing the luminosity of his state of moral elevation. He spoke with beautiful vocal intonation:

"Dear brothers and sisters:
"May Jesus, the Sublime Guide of Humanity, bless us.
"Not long ago, our plans were merely outlined possibilities, but now they are a reality, thanks to the devotion of sincere servants of the Good.

"Several groups of workers of the Gospel on our plane descended to the earth in order to create conditions for building the Kingdom of Heaven in people's hearts. Now they have returned to our community, leaving room for other workers to continue the plan, which will be fulfilled according to the results achieved in the initial experiences.

"We happily foresee the future days of the planet's complete moral renewal as low order spirits are relocated to other worlds, where they will continue the progress they have denied themselves till now, and as the messengers of the Light transform the mechanisms of war into instruments of peace, and those of vice and crime into love and liberation.

"The workers of the great transformation have been operating diligently in the various social and cultural segments of the earth for some time now.

"Great migrations of happy spirits interested in changing the world's social structures for the better, when suffering will flee in shame because its presence is no longer needed, are taking place.

"The promise of Jesus concerning the world of regeneration on its way to being a paradise or a happy planet is now feasible as selfless workers from the spirit world prepare the environment where these builders of tomorrow will live.

"We congratulate our dear brothers and sisters who are now closing their tour of fraternity after the period granted to them for the execution of the endeavor.

"Since there is no rest in the form of idleness here, after a brief period of renewal and study, they will return to the earth for further spiritual responsibilities, contributing more effectively in an attempt to awaken the rebellious and the insane so that they may be given the opportunity for repentance and moral rectification, instead of the exile that would otherwise be imposed on them by the Divine Law.

"Of course these activities will be more painful and challenging than those carried out during the period now ending.

"We trust that the Sublime Worker will equip us with the resources and tools needed to carry out the future plan as successfully as the one just completed.

"May He Himself, our Example and Model, lead us with His love – that is the prayer of your devoted and faithful friend."

When he finished, we again heard the angelic music and children's voices singing hosannas to Jesus and life.

He returned to the cylinder and dissolved before our dewy eyes...

Then Dr. Santana stood up to thank all who had been part of his team.

With a choked voice, he prayed:

Beloved Master Jesus:

You invited us to work in Your harvest. Completely unequipped, we presented ourselves at the last hour, when You welcomed us and offered us a field to plow.

Although the day was spent and the night approached, You have allowed us to hurry and plow the fields of hardened hearts so that we may sow Your word of love and light in them.

Even after our earlier failures, You did not hesitate to grant us the ballast of confidence to implement Your plan for the earth's renewal, despite our little experience and very little wisdom.

In spite of our fighting against our imperfections, You visited us countless times to sustain us in our effort of self-transformation for the better so that we can face our inner challenges and solve outer difficulties.

The days have passed in the hourglass of time and we have reached the final stage with hands almost empty of deeds, but with our hearts and minds thankful for all Your wonderful gifts.

Forgive us for our inadequacy, limitations and difficulties, but what we do have we offer in service to You, and what we would love to accomplish, we try to do it, being at Your disposal for future endeavors.

Honor us with new callings and enrich us with Your incomparable mercy, providing us new commitments of light.

We thank You, our Lord, depositing in Your loving heart our best sentiments of tenderness and gratitude.

When he finished, the emotions had reached their peak.

The wonderful meeting had ended and the time for farewells had come.

All the aspects of the endeavor passed through my mind and emotions, from the first stage with the victims of the Indian Ocean tsunami, to our helping the young medium, and concluding with the victory of love in all its expressions.

A new day was dawning when our caravan, still under the command of Dr. Silvio Santana, returned to our spirit plane.

As we got farther away from the beloved earth, we could see it enveloped in blue light, swirling in the cosmos and advancing in the direction of a *planet of regeneration*.

Ivon Costa

Ivon Costa was born in São Manuel, today Eugenópolis, in Minas Gerais, Brazil, on July 15, 1898, and discarnated in Porto Alegre (Rio Grande do Sul) on January 9, 1934, at only 35 years old. He was one of the most noteworthy Spiritist speakers in Brazil and contributed decisively with his insightful and enlightening word to further the spread of the Spiritist Doctrine with unbreakable fiber and true valor.

He was endowed with an enviable gift of oratory and possessed an infectious magnetism and a privileged voice, keeping his audiences spellbound with the force of his argument.

He was a seminary student at one time, but with only 19 days remaining until his ordination as a priest, it was discovered that he had no baptismal certificate. In light of the confusion, Ivon gave up his ecclesiastical career.

He moved to Rio de Janeiro, where he graduated in medicine. He was a remarkable polyglot, speaking perfect French, English, German and Spanish.

At one point, when he was going through a difficult phase in his life, he found himself in front of a Spiritist center that was holding a public meeting. Moved by an odd impulse, he went in and listened to comments on the Codification by

Allan Kardec. When he left, he was transformed because he had found the answer to all his questions.

He became a Spiritist and soon took up the task of lecturer. Possessing solid intellectual knowledge, in addition to being a medium, he stood out with rare brilliance at the podium. He also engaged in dialogue with the audience in order further clarify the arguments presented in conferences.

He also toured countries in Europe, including Portugal, Spain, France, Holland, Belgium and Luxembourg.

On one occasion he was to give a lecture in Maceió, Brazil in a rented theater, but just before the conference, the theater was closed by order of the local bishop. The public, unhappy with the attitude of the clergyman, led Ivon to the square, where the lecture was held. In retaliation, the church bells tolled and some fanatics pelted him with stones; however, he endured all stoically and with a true spirit of selflessness.

Ivon Costa lived two years in Germany before moving to Paris, where he served as a cinematic interpreter for Paramount. Everywhere he went, he planted the seeds of the Doctrine of the Spirits (Spiritism). He also attended the International Congress on Spiritism in The Hague, Netherlands.

In 1932 he returned to Brazil for good, settling in Porto Alegre, where he ran a free clinic.

We can affirm that Ivon Costa was the first Spiritist who traveled the most in order to spread the reincarnationist ideals, and this endeavor was very similar to that performed by the great lecturers Vianna de Carvalho and Divaldo Franco.

His missionary work resulted in the founding of a large number of Spiritist societies throughout Brazil.

Made in the USA
Lexington, KY
09 November 2016